Music for All

Developing music in the curriculum with pupils with special educational needs

Peter Wills & Melanie Peter

**Advisory Teachers
for the Arts
Norfolk LEA**

David Fulton Publishers
London

David Fulton Publishers Ltd
2 Barbon Close, London WC1N 3JX

First published in Great Britain by
David Fulton Publishers 1996

Note: The right of the authors to be identified as the authors of their work has been asserted by them in accordance with the Copyright, Designs and Patents Act 1988.

Copyright © Norfolk County Council Inspection, Advice and Training Services

British Library Cataloguing in Publication Data

A catalogue record for this book is available from the British Library

ISBN 1-85346-280-2

All rights reserved. No part of this publication may be reproduced, stored in a retrieval system or transmitted, in any form, or by any means, electronic, mechanical, photocopying, recording or otherwise, without the prior permission of the publishers.

Typeset by The Harrington Consultancy Ltd
Printed in Great Britain by Bell and Bain Ltd, Glasgow

Contents

	Acknowledgements	iv
	Introduction	v
1	Music in the Curriculum	1
2	Preparing for Music in the Classroom	8
3	Planning Classroom Music	18
4	Building Blocks – The Elements for Music-making	33
5	Towards Composition – Structuring Music	51
6	Learning to Listen – Listening to and Appraising Music	60
	Resources	73
	Bibliography	75

DEDICATION
To the pupils and staff in Norfolk's special schools

Acknowledgements

This handbook is the result of a collaborative venture between members of Norfolk's Arts in Education Service, one arm of Norfolk LEA's Inspection, Advice and Training Services. The team of advisory teachers in the arts put together a package of in-service training programmes to meet the needs of teachers working in Norfolk's special schools. It was known as The EASE project – Educating in the Arts in Special Education. Teachers were concerned that their pupils with learning difficulties should have their entitlement to a developmental arts education in the light of the National Curriculum. As a result, this handbook was spawned, to enable teachers to access learning programmes in music in small steps, with the needs of those pupils with learning difficulties particularly in mind.

As joint authors, we are indebted to the support of Norfolk LEA for commissioning this handbook. We have learned an enormous amount from having the opportunity to work together and pool our respective expertise and experience, gleaned from our backgrounds in the fields of music and special education. We are grateful to staff and pupils amongst Norfolk's special schools for all their support and enthusiasm for our work. We'd like to thank Derek Paice for his contribution to the book on Music Technology, an area in which he has particular interest and expertise. We'd also like to thank Jillian Tearoe for her assistance with the recording profiles, and for her administrative support, together with Paula Stubbs.

Finally, we owe personal thanks to our colleagues within the Arts in Education Service for all the stimulating debates around issues arising from the handbook – to Keith Winser, Polly Plowman, Derek Paice, Beatrice Hoffman, Tony Taylor and especially our manager David Sheppard. We couldn't wish for better 'critical friends'!

Peter Wills and Melanie Peter
Autumn 1995

Note: Norfolk's Arts in Education Service offers a wide range of consultancy, advice, support and training in all aspects of the arts in education. Readers interested in other services are invited to write for further details, to: David Sheppard, Centre for the Arts in Education, Bull Close Road, Norwich NR3 1NG.

Introduction

Music is a life-enriching experience for all members of society. It is widely recognised that music is a powerful means of communication and expression. This makes it a particularly pertinent medium when working with people with wide-ranging learning difficulties. The tradition of music as *therapy* with people with special needs is well established, with connotations of 'helping and healing'. This book, however, seeks to place music in an *educational* context. It offers a practical approach to the teaching of music to pupils with wide-ranging learning needs. It presents a developmental framework for structuring progressively more challenging music activity, to enable pupils of all abilities to progress in sufficiently small steps so that their achievements may be recognised. It explains how to make possible the notion of 'music for all'.

Music for All presents a *framework* and guidelines for planning music lessons with pupils with learning difficulties within the requirements of the National Curriculum. As well as illustrations of good practice, ideas and examples of lessons and activities are offered as *suggestions* and as starting-points for teachers' own lesson ideas. They will need to be applied sensitively according to their relevance for meeting the needs of individual pupils. Examples are *not* intended to be used 'once and forever' – rather, activities may need repeating time and again, adapting and embellishing to provide *breadth* of experience. This raises the issue of what constitutes progress in music: is it being able to do things that are increasingly complex? Or is it being able to do the same thing but better? Or the same thing, but with increasing awareness and understanding?

Chapter 1 discusses music in the curriculum. It considers the aims of music-in-education and discusses the thinking behind National Curriculum documentation – issues relating to the development of pupils' sensitivity, understanding and enjoyment of music, through active involvement in listening, composing and performing. It looks at implications for delivering and accessing music activity to pupils with a range of learning difficulties, to enable them to achieve and experience quality teaching and learning. A key factor in pupils' music development will be the ability of the teacher to plan and present appropriately differentiated music activities that will enable *all* pupils to progress by meeting individual needs within the context of the group. The rest of the book endeavours to show how this may be achieved.

The teacher will need to ensure access to an appropriate range of resources to support developmentally appropriate music activity. Chapter 2 suggests how to organise classroom instruments in a way that will present pupils with suitable challenges, whilst enabling the creative process to flourish. The contribution of music technology and IT in music education has become widely recognised in recent years. Our colleague **Derek Paice** outlines its possible uses for enhancing the musical potential of pupils with a range of learning difficulties.

Planning classroom music will need to reflect the development of individual pupils within the context of the group experience. Chapter 3 discusses a framework for structuring a music lesson, taking account of music aims and objectives for the *group* and how these can be developed and explored. It suggests evaluative procedures for the teacher for reflecting on the effectiveness of teaching strategies, and for informing future work. Examples of lessons are provided, carried out with pupils across the age and ability range, typical of a special educational setting. They are designed to indicate pupils' growing maturity and development in different aspects of music education to meet National Curriculum requirements.

The National Curriculum states that performing and composing, and listening to and appraising music should be mutually reinforcing and inter-related within classroom music activities. However, whilst empowering in its intention, further guidance may be required for teachers working with pupils with learning difficulties, who may be progressing in very small steps. An individual pupil may have a very 'patchy' profile in the different aspects of music, and the differences between individual members of the group may vary even more. In order to meet individual needs, the teacher will have to identify and plan for progress in the different areas of music education for *all* members of the group. The teacher will need to take account of progress also in terms of *breadth* of experience, particularly for those pupils who may 'plateau' at a stage of development for a long time. Therefore, it is helpful to isolate those distinct aspects of development in music, so that the teacher may offer truly differentiated work.

Chapters 4, 5 and 6 tackle individual progress in the acknowledged areas of music education: the elements for music-making, structuring music and appreciating music through active listening. These three strands reflect the Programmes of Study across the Key stages in the National Curriculum (DFE, 1995). Chapter 4 examines progress in the 'building blocks' for music-making – the essential music elements on which all subsequent music activity is based. Chapter 5 suggests a developmental framework for enabling pupils to work towards composition, through increasingly challenging musical structures, with consideration for performing with and to others. Chapter 6 proposes strategies for enabling pupils to learn to listen to music from a range of cultures and traditions, with growing understanding and appreciation.

In considering progression in music with the needs of pupils of *all* abilities in mind, we found ourselves caught up in the inherent contradiction within the National Curriculum with regard to pupils with special educational needs. Teachers are exhorted to select developmentally-appropriate material for their pupils from Programmes of Study across the Key stages. However, this does not escape the difficulty that these are effectively age-related, and therefore indicative of pupils' development against expectations of a national 'norm'. Furthermore, teachers are required to map their pupils' achievements against End of Key Stage Descriptions (EKSDs). EKSDs are intended to reflect notional levels of attainment (eg Level 2 at Key stage 1, and Level 4 at the end of Key stage 2); this risks disadvantaging pupils with learning difficulties, as their achievements may be regarded negatively.

A central dilemma for us as authors, therefore, has been the indication of benchmarks of development in music. How should we identify them? Pupils with learning difficulties may pass through the same developmental stages as their mainstream peers, although their actual chronological ages may differ. In practice, however, teachers tend to be aware of how criterion-referenced aims and objectives actually link with developmental 'norms'. Given the intention of the National Curriculum to be enabling, empowering and 'normalising', we have compromised, in order to assist teachers in planning for individual needs within the context of the group: the difficulty being that music lessons are usually planned as a *group* experience.

We have identified four distinct, recognisable stages of development in music, which we have termed 'reactive', 'active', 'interactive' and 'proactive'. We have indicated how individual aims and objectives may dovetail with developmentally-appropriate activities, to correlate with material in National Curriculum Programmes of Study, equivalent to progression through Key stages 1 and 2/3. These have been further sub-divided into lower and upper stages to assist teachers planning for *breadth* of development for groups of pupils progressing in small steps, and also to indicate how pupils may be challenged *within* a particular Key stage. Individual objectives address patterns of development in the different aspects of music: identifiable criteria towards achieving long-term aims in making, composing and listening to music. These represent a convenient but arbitrary blueprint of six sub-stages, as might be expected within a special educational setting catering for pupils with a range of learning difficulties. As such, they may assist teachers in differentiating music work to meet individual needs within group activity. Pupils with special educational needs may have patchy profiles: a pupil may be at different developmental stages in the various aspects of music.

Even the most severely disabled member of society may be enabled to share in creative musical experiences. Activities in school may be just the start of their broadening awareness of music – class-based lessons, multi-class or whole-school events, concerts and visiting musicians. Pupils' interest may be expanded through exploring and exploiting musical opportunities out of the immediate school environment, by making full use of resources and facilities in the community. For example, visits to concerts, community music groups, resources in neighbouring schools, arts centres, etc. Occasionally individual pupils (even with severe learning difficulties) may demonstrate exceptional *ability* in music. Teachers need to be alert to drawing on the expertise, advice and tuition of music specialists – initially by contacting arts-in-education services and advisers. It may be that peripatetic music staff can be employed in school to work with pupils, as well as advisory teachers offering advice and support to staff. Additionally, individual and group music therapy may complement existing music work in schools.

Most importantly, music should be pleasurable for all concerned. Gone are the days when we could cheerfully say to colleagues 'be brave, give it a go!'. Nowadays schools are statutorily obliged to deliver a music curriculum, whether a staff considers itself 'musical' or not. We hope we have gone some way towards demystifying the National Curriculum Music Order (DFE, 1995) and using stipulated requirements as a springboard for enriching classroom music with pupils of all abilities. Whilst the book has been written in support of pupils with learning difficulties, effectively it breaks down National Curriculum Programmes of Study in Music up to the end of Key stage 2 into manageable, identifiable stages. We hope, therefore, that teachers both in mainstream primary as well as in special education will find relevance and use in *Music for All*. Hopefully it will provide sufficient guidance for the 'musically challenged' – teachers as well as pupils! After all, 'enjoyment' is now statutory (DFE, 1995)!

We hear a song coming on …!

CHAPTER 1

Music in the Curriculum

This chapter will consider the aims of music education in the light of the National Curriculum requirements, and propose strategies for structuring music activity towards enabling pupils of all abilities to have access to their entitlement. It represents a mainstream approach to music in education, with consideration for the particular challenges presented by pupils with wide-ranging needs.

Aims of Music Education Issues relating to methodology and practicalities of delivering stipulated requirements have largely been removed from the revised National Curriculum Music Order (DFE, 1995). Earlier documentation stated the main aim for music education as being:

> ... to foster pupils' sensitivity to, and their understanding and enjoyment of music, through an active involvement in listening, composing and performing (NCC, 1991, 4.3, p7).

The NCC (1991) recognises the development of musical perception and skills as being dependent on the quality, range and appropriateness of these musical experiences. It acknowledges the range of different forms of musical expression, and that notions of excellence may be found in any musical style. In particular, it considers that progress in music should cover the development of:

- awareness and appreciation of organised sound patterns;
- skills in movement, such as motor co-ordination and dexterity, vocal skills and skills in aural imagery (imagining and internalising sounds), acquired through exploring and organising sound;
- sensitive, analytical and critical responses to music;
- the capacity to express ideas, thoughts and feeling through music;
- awareness and understanding of tradition, idioms and musical styles from a variety of cultures, times and places;

- the experience of fulfilment which derives from the highest possible artistic and technical standards (NCC, 1991, 4.4, p7).

Additionally, the contribution of music to the whole curriculum is recognised, by developing in pupils the following essentially transferable skills and attributes:

- delight in a sense of individual and collective achievement;
- aesthetic appreciation and discrimination;
- listening skills and sensitivity to sounds;
- imagination and inventiveness;
- intellectual and artistic skills;
- the ability to analyse and solve problems;
- study skills, including attention to detail, lengthened attention span, concern for accuracy, memorising and the interpretation of sounds and symbols;
- communication skills (non-verbal as well as verbal);
- social skills, such as co-operation, resourcefulness, perseverance, tolerance and self-confidence;
- self-motivation, self-discipline, self-analysis and self-evaluation;
- awareness and appreciation of a wide range of cultural traditions (NCC, 1991, 4.13, p8).

OFSTED (1993) also recognises the value of music in contributing to the development of pupils' spiritual, moral, social and cultural development; for example, music may expose pupils to a range of cultural traditions, and foster respect and appreciation of different musical styles and the accomplishments of others. The NCC (1991) recognises that the making and understanding of music share certain processes with other arts, in particular dance and/or drama. Some activities may be planned in a co-ordinated way to address both areas of learning. Cross-arts activities may be mutually enhancing and enriching; for example, pupils in Key stages 1 and 2 will often respond to music naturally through movement.

Music and Pupils with Special Educational Needs

Whilst some of the above aims at first reading may appear rather grand in relation to the abilities of certain pupils, the intention behind the Music Order is nevertheless meant to be enabling. The NCC (1991) makes specific reference to the entitlement of *all* pupils:

> 4.5 Pupils of all levels of ability should be able to develop [these] skills and capacities, gain understanding of musical elements, and realise their creativity, by engaging in musical activities in a planned and structured way. They should be encouraged, at the same time, to develop the open-minded, yet sensitive and discriminating attitudes which music education seeks to foster (NCC, 1991, p7).

Music may contribute to breaking down barriers between pupils and releasing potential within them. However, with regard to pupils with learning difficulties:

> a) **pupils** may need positive steering towards experiences and activities in which they can succeed;

b) the **tasks** towards which pupils are steered may need to be adapted to enable them to respond positively;

c) additional **resources** may be needed if we are to ensure equal opportunities for all pupils (NCC, 1991, 11.2, p51).

Differentiating the curriculum

This should be the means by which *all* pupils may be enabled to participate in music work, taking account of their individual needs and abilities. A range of classroom strategies may be used in music work with groups with diverse needs:

- Resources may be presented with inherent, developmentally-appropriate challenges for pupils of all abilities (the 'wallet' principle, of a collection of items); for example, instruments available may include some that are suitable for pupils at both extremes of the ability range, as well as those in between (see chapter 2).
- In structuring music work, the teacher may allocate specific tasks to challenge pupils according to their respective abilities, which may then be combined to create a group piece which harnesses the contribution of everyone (a 'jigsaw' approach); for example, a group composition may require some pupils to play a continuous background sound on shakers, others to maintain a pulse on percussion instruments, others to play a rhythmic ostinato (musical pattern) on unpitched instruments, others to wait and play at a specific moment on cue.
- An activity may be 'layered', with differing challenges presented to extend pupils according to their ability; for example, when listening to a piece of music, some pupils may be expected to respond to its mood by moving spontaneously, others may be asked to listen for a particular familiar sound or a notable contrast in the music (eg when the singing starts, sudden loud moments, etc), others may be asked to comment on how the musical elements are used (eg texture – solo or group playing? tempo – fast or slow sections? etc), others to comment on its evocative quality or particular use of certain sounds (eg does it remind them of anything? which instruments played the quiet moments? etc).
- Several points of entry may be used into the same activity ('differentiation by task'), where the responsibility is on the pupils to create within the parameters defined by the teacher; for example, an exercise on chime bars may require some pupils to play a single bar, others to alternate playing using two beaters on two chime bars, others to maintain an ostinato (musical pattern) on three or more chosen bars, others to pick out and play required notes from a full scale of eight chime bars.
- The same activity may be delivered to different pupils, with varying responses according to their respective ability ('differentiation by outcome'); for example, accompanying a song with contrasting loud and quiet sections using percussion may prompt some pupils to 'play along' freely, others to adapt playing recognising an extreme change in dynamics (loud or quiet), others to play a crescendo recognising when the music is gradually getting louder, others to play a crescendo and diminuendo adjusting playing to get louder and softer accordingly.
- Different methods of learning style may need to be used in order to access

aspects of the music curriculum to pupils; for example, recording a composition that tells a story in sound may require certain pupils to capture their playing on tape, others to use pictorial images (eg placing picture cards in a sequence to reflect their playing), others to relate to graphic symbols (eg writing patterns to represent particular instruments), others to relate to symbols that indicate how as well as when to play (eg for getting louder, quieter, faster, slower, etc).
- Evaluating work should take account of the extent to which achievements of individual pupils reflect their expected potential, with the efforts of all pupils valued with regard to their respective stage of development in the different aspects of making, composing and listening to music.

As the NCC (1991) states, teachers will need, therefore, to be specially aware of the *abilities* rather than the disabilities of children with special educational needs, and to identify those points across the attainment targets which will best allow the pupils:

- to experience a sense of achievement and worth;
- to develop confidence;
- to make an identifiable individual contribution; and
- to be sensitive to the musical activities and creation of others (p52).

Accessing the curriculum

End of Key Stage Descriptions (DFE, 1995) are intended essentially as a reporting tool, to be interpreted flexibly, with the intention that these will be wholly or in part accessible to *all* pupils at the relevant age range. Aims and objectives in music, however, should be identified in relation to Programme Of Study (POS) most relevant for the pupils' ability across the Key stages, in order for pupils to progress and demonstrate achievement, with the proviso that material is presented in contexts suitable to their actual chronological age. What is required, therefore, is the identification of *sub-stages* towards achieving stated goals, in order to recognise and plan for achievement in pupils progressing in small steps. Additionally, teachers may need to plan for *breadth* of experience, for pupils who may remain at a particular stage of development for a long time.

The teacher working with a group of pupils with learning difficulties will need to be equipped and prepared to cater for wide-ranging individual needs within the context of the group. A *multi-sensory* approach may be adopted, in order for pupils to learn through their most effective means and to work to their relative strengths and abilities. It may be necessary to explore a range of means to present the same material to different pupils. For example, a deaf child may experience music not only through visual reinforcement with a strong visual stimulus (eg a brightly coloured or appealing instrument), but also through feeling vibrations; a blind pupil in the same group will also experience music through vibration, but may require more tactile reinforcement of a teaching point.

The National Curriculum (DFE, 1995) makes specific mention of the need for appropriate provision for pupils with physical and sensory disabilities, to enable them to participate in music work, using technological aids and equipment, and alternative means of communication and of acquiring information. NASEN (1992, p11–12) lists examples of practical ways in which diverse needs may be accommodated within classroom music:

The un-co-ordinated child will need:

- additional time to practise a skill;
- a suitable musical instrument which is easy to play:
  a) an instrument which can be played with one hand (eg a cymbal played with a soft beater; a hand chime instead of a chime bar or glockenspiel);
  b) a percussion instrument with a large playing surface;
  c) an instrument which is supported in a position which is convenient for playing (eg a triangle suspended on a music stand);
  d) a recorder with a thumb-hole with sellotape, or a one-handed recorder.
- gradually to progress musically from playing an instrument with one hand to two hands, eg:
  – playing bongo drums with two hands;
  – playing bongo drums with two sticks;
  – playing one chime bar with one stick;
  – playing two chime bars placed far apart with one stick;
  – playing a xylophone, crossing mid-line; etc.

The child with breathing problems should be allowed:

- to play a swanee-whistle, kazoo, recorder or ocarina;
- eventually to learn an orchestral wind instrument (woodwind or brass).

The physically-disabled child is likely to need:

- an instrument specifically designed or adapted to his/her specific needs (see above);
- an instrument suitably supported (see above);
- an electronic keyboard, drum machine, etc.

The hearing-impaired child will need:

- a quiet learning environment;
- an instrument in which vibrations can be felt;
- a low or high pitched instrument, according to his/her specific needs;
- a sprung wooden floor to lie on in order to experience a greatly increased sensation of vibration.

The visually-impaired child will need to be given:

- a seat with a good view;
- plenty of time to practise a skill;
- music which can be learned by rote;
- music with notation which is larger than usual;
- white notes on a black background if necessary;
- an instrument which can be played by feel, eg a maraca, castanet or recorder;
- a sighted partner with whom to play.

The child with learning difficulties needs:

- relevant teaching techniques with clear instruction;
- repetition in all phases of work with visual sign symbols and clues;
- plenty of encouragement.

The child with severe learning difficulties should have:

- the opportunity to use Makaton signing when learning a song, eg signs on the first beat of a bar, songs for linking signs.

The child with emotional or behavioural difficulties will need to be given:

- regular exposure to a variety of musical activities (this also applies to all other children with special educational needs);
- his or her own personal space in which to work;
- enjoyable activities which have specific rules and clear instructions;
- an instrument which is appropriate to his/her own abilities, eg one which is easy to play and easy to keep silent;
- structured opportunities to experiment;
- plenty of encouragement and praise.

The child who is musically more able will need:

- encouragement to proceed at his/her own pace;
- specialist help in order that his/her talents can be fully developed;
- the benefit of expertise from neighbouring primary or secondary schools;
- opportunities to gain confidence by playing to, and helping (for example) slower learners (musically speaking).

Implications for Teaching and Learning in Music

The following pointers are based on criteria for achievement and quality of teaching and learning in music identified by OFSTED (1993), but with particular reference to working with pupils with learning difficulties:

- Pupils need to develop technical control both of instruments and their voices: where possible, pupils of all abilities should be extended with increasingly challenging instruments to be shaken, tapped, scraped and blown (see chapter 2), and develop their vocal range and its powers of expression.
- Pupils need to learn to use music to communicate expressively, to select and organise sounds and musical ideas with developing imagination: pupils should be offered clear parameters within which to create, which may be gradually broadened – paradoxically, *limiting* choices initially may enable certain pupils with learning difficulties to respond to tasks, and to learn to engage in creative decision-making in music.
- Pupils need to be aware of the interrelationship of performing, composing, listening and appraising: teachers need to develop strategies for active listening, in a way that directly relates to pupils' own music-making and compositions – teachers of pupils with learning difficulties may need to use a range of visual aids and/or multi-sensory devices as 'hooks' or prompts, to enable pupils to make connections and to focus their attention.
- Pupils should be encouraged to respond to music they have listened to and

composed, to ask as well as answer questions, and to develop a musical vocabulary; also to write their responses if appropriate – teachers may need to be flexible in their interpretations of the reactions to music of certain pupils with learning difficulties, accepting non-verbal responses, and posing questions that may be answered with a yes/no (see chapter 6).

- Individual pupil needs should be accommodated within the context of the group experience; this may necessitate the teacher of pupils with very diverse needs being highly organised to provide opportunities for each pupil to progress, with in-depth knowledge of stages of development in different aspects of making, composing and listening to music, in order to differentiate activities.

- Sequences of lessons should be planned to reflect general requirements for the National Curriculum Programmes of Study: pupils of all abilities will need to be offered a balance between activities that are familiar, in which they may confidently improve their skills and develop their awareness and understanding in activities they recognise, and also be challenged in new and/or increasingly complex activities in which their musical skills may be extended.

- Pupils may need to develop work at differing rates, at a pace that allows them to consolidate learning, with recognition that work may need to be carried over from session to session: lessons should be sufficiently long to allow pupils to explore aspects of music in depth, and sufficiently frequent to capitalise and build on learning in the light of National Curriculum requirements – it may be preferable to spread one lesson over two or more sessions rather than rush, perhaps with 'work in progress' stored on tape (see chapter 3).

- Assessment of the achievements of pupils in making, composing and listening to music, should take account of the full range of their experience, including beyond classroom music: planning for and recognising the breadth of pupils' experience will be particularly significant for those pupils with learning difficulties remaining at a stage of development for a long time; teachers will also need to be aware of sub-stages towards achieving goals in making, composing and listening to music (see chapters 4, 5 and 6), and to differentiate activities accordingly to make it possible for pupils to achieve.

- Music theory should be taught only in a musical context, as an integral part of music work – teaching traditional notation (dots on a stave), in any case, may well be inappropriate for many mainstream primary pupils, let alone those pupils with learning difficulties; however, the ability of *all* pupils should be developed in performing and composing music using other forms of notation, and also by ear, even if this requires imagination and flexibility on the part of the teacher, to develop strategies to make this possible (see chapters 4 and 5).

CHAPTER 2

Preparing for Music in the Classroom

This chapter will suggest ways to manage classroom resources to support the delivery of the music curriculum to pupils with learning difficulties. It will consider suitable instruments for developing the musical skills of pupils across the age and ability range. It will also look at possible ways to use music technology to enhance pupils' musical creativity, in a section written by Derek Paice.

In addition to conventional instruments, useful resources for music may include some or all of the following:

- a cassette player, with recording and tape counter facilities;
- a supply of blank tapes for recording pupils' own music-making;
- a range of prerecorded music in different styles and from different cultures and times;
- experimental sound makers from found sources – eg dry chicken bones, coconut shells, empty yogurt pots, walnut shells, stones, metal trays, etc;
- instruments made by pupils from a range of materials;
- visual stimuli to support and reinforce musical ideas – eg a range of pictures (common objects, animals and images from the environment) which can be represented in sound;
- large sheets of paper and thick coloured pens for producing a musical score;
- access to a range of appropriate music technology.

Classroom Instruments   A glance through many educational catalogues will reveal a bewildering array of instruments available for school use. Cheap toy instruments will have a limited life and, whilst appealing and fun to play with, ultimately will have limited potential for music making. In order to provide musical experiences, instruments need to be:

- good quality;
- durable;
- attractive;
- in good repair;
- safe.

The range of instruments offered at any stage of development will need to present possibilities for:

- creating sounds in different ways – shaking, tapping, blowing, scraping;
- producing different dynamics – loud, quiet, etc;
- varying sound qualities – wooden and metal instruments, with a selection of beaters of varying hardness (hard, medium, soft): sticks, beaters, brushes in wood, plastic, metal, etc;
- exploring high and low sounds, including pitched instruments (xylophones, glockenspiels, metallophones, chime bars, keyboard, etc);
- making long and short sounds – ringing, echoing, reverberating, clipped, etc.

It is important to consider *how* and *why* an instrument is being used at any stage of a pupil's development. Whilst pupils will need access to a range of instruments, their introduction needs to be phased. Pupils need to be offered a balance between instruments with which they are familiar in order to develop their confidence and proficiency in playing, and also sufficient variety with 'new' or unfamiliar instruments to enrich and extend their musical experience. Some instruments are inherently less demanding to play, and are therefore more suitable for developmentally young pupils, whilst others present more challenges in terms of their complexity or motoric skill required to play them. Pupils with limited physical abilities will need instruments adapted and presented in a way that will enable them to achieve success; for example, a cymbal or windchimes suspended on a stand within range of the pupil, and use of enlarged/padded grips on beaters. Pupils' musical experience may also be extended through teachers and supporting staff playing more demanding instruments, including orchestral instruments. Pupils need to develop an awareness of possibilities and the potential of different instruments in order to be able to make informed choices for their own music making.

Very often musical instruments in schools tend to be stored on a trolley, with resources shared between classes around the school. Additionally, classes may have a more limited selection of basic percussion instruments. Ideally, these should all be organised so that staff and pupils can select appropriate instruments; for example, separate crates or boxes for blowing, tapping, shaking, scraping and pitched sounds. These could be labelled pictorially, so that instruments may be returned by all involved (staff and pupils) to the appropriate container. If these are to be shared around the school, then staff need to be aware that not all the instruments in the crates will necessarily be appropriate for their particular pupils' stage of development. Staff may wish to consider 'holding back' certain instruments so that pupils are increasingly offered more sophisticated instruments as they progress through the school. For example, a shekere (fragile gourd shaker) may be more suitable for older pupils offered as a regularly available choice, but may be introduced selectively lower down the school with staff support for novelty. Teachers will need to organise instruments ahead of the session, selecting appropriate instruments for their pupils, so that they are able to draw from a suitable range.

Alternatively classes may equip themselves with basic percussion kits, and opt to have a central stock of more exotic and pitched instruments. Ideally, these should still all be organised according to the skill required to play them. Instruments to be stored centrally could include the following: bodhran (large Irish tambour), individual chime bars, bass, alto and soprano metallophones, xylophones and glockenspiels; gato drums, rainmaker tubes, shekere, afuche de coco, gong, drum kit, conga drum(s), temple blocks, vibraslap, wind chimes, tubular bells, crash cymbal on stand, snare drum on stand, tabla drums, talking drum, kalimba (thumb piano), pocket rattle, kokoriko, recorders and melodicas, set of individual hand bells/chimes, panpipes, individual toned horns (as used at the Nordoff Robbins Music Therapy Institute).

Teachers should be aware of enabling pupils to progress in controlling sounds, through presenting appropriately challenging instruments in class activities. We offer the following suggestions for pacing and differentiating the introduction of a range of instruments. This should not be adhered to rigidly, but should be adapted and extended according to the abilities and needs of the pupils and the sounds required. For example, whilst jingle bells on a ring may seem unsophisticated for senior age pupils, it may be just the effect they desire to achieve a wintery sound in their composition. Initially, teachers need to select instruments according to the developmental needs of the pupils, in terms of their ability to *handle* them and *control* their sounds. Instruments will then need to be further organised according to their musical *effect* – for example, wooden, metal and reverberating sounds (the quality of which will be influenced by the manufacture).

Lower Key stage 1 (including nursery/reception/pupils with PMLD)

Pupils need 'hands on' playing of instruments where possible with or without teacher support in order to explore and discover possibilities with a range of sounds. This may be extended further through listening to staff playing more complex instruments. Pupils' attention may need to be gained through the visual and tactile appeal of the instrument, for example an intriguing large transparent 'rainmaker tube' or 'ocean drum', where it is possible to watch the contents moving. It is possible to obtain sturdy basic percussion instruments which have been designed specifically with the needs of developmentally young musicians in mind; for example, finger castanets with animal faces, myna bird slide whistles, etc. Whilst instruments may need to be light enough for pupils to hold independently (especially those pupils with weak wrist strength), it may also be the case that they require a large playing surface offered by more substantial instruments, which will need to be supported (on a stand or held by a member of staff).

Instruments available for exploration may include:

- *shaking instruments:* small hand held instruments, including maracas, different types of bells, single and multiple ankle and wrist bells, coloured bells mounted on a rotating frame, coloured egg shakers, noise-makers from found sources, crescent tambourine, rainmaker tube, ocean drum;
- *tapping instruments:* (played with the flat hand or an adapted beater as necessary): claves, drum, tambour, tambourine, castanets (finger or table-mounted), gong, cymbal, ocean drum;
- *scraping instruments:* sand paper blocks (possibly on sock worn on the whole hand), finger nails across a skin drum or tambour, guiro, small stick dragged across a range of surfaces;
- *blowing instruments* (for those pupils with sufficient control of their breath

and the lip, tongue and cheek muscles): myna bird slide whistles, kazoo, whistle (NB with attention to health and safety issues);
- *pitched instruments:* individual chime bars, individual large tone bars, two-tone whistle, cuckoo call, ocarina, wind chimes.

Upper Key stage 1

Instruments for pupils at this stage should offer independence in controlling and managing sounds. Sounds need to be easily achieved with minimal effort from those pupils with limited strength; other pupils will need to learn to control the amount of energy they need to exert and to acquire a sense of 'fine touch'. Instruments will need to be sufficiently resilient to withstand allcomers! Additionally, instruments will need to present pupils with the challenge of requiring a greater degree of co-ordination; for example, those instruments played with a beater.

Instruments available for exploration may include all the above, in addition:

- *shaking instruments:* maracas, jingle sticks, jingle bells, handled castanets, pocket rattle;
- *tapping instruments:* two-tone wood block, single wood blocks of different sizes, single wooden agogo, double wooden agogo, tulip block, tongue drum, wooden octachime, tambourine with beater, triangle, finger cymbals, hand cymbals;
- *scraping instruments:* multi guiro, double wooden agogo, scraper board, wooden xylophone 'ribs' mounted on string worn round the neck;
- *blowing instruments:* toy symphony trumpet, swanee whistle, duck call, cuckoo call, toned whistles;
- *pitched instruments:* chime bar step ladder, hand held chime tree, up-ended alto xylophone and/or metallophone, swanee whistle.

Lower Key stage 2

By this stage, pupils need to be challenged with instruments that may be played with more subtlety to achieve a range of musical effects and dynamics. Pupils in the main will be physically larger, therefore capable of managing larger instruments as well as small ones. Opportunities should be offered for them to play the same instrument of varied sizes; for example, different sized triangles, tambours, etc. In addition, they may be challenged with instruments that are more demanding in terms of the degree of co-ordination and manipulative skill required to play them appropriately; for example, a cabasa, nightingale call, two or more chime bars, etc. More unusual instruments may be introduced at this stage, to encourage pupils to transfer and generalise playing skills of tapping, shaking, scraping and blowing – for example, an afuche de coco. Additionally, certain instruments may be presented that inherently pose challenges of control; for example, metal instruments will need to be played quietly, and those that are more fragile (eg a gourd shekere) will also require a degree of care and responsibility as well as 'fine touch'.

Instruments available for exploration may include all the above, in addition:

- *shaking instruments:* metal shaker, slap stick, football rattle, pocket rattle, kokiriko, cabasa, afuche, flexatone;
- *tapping instruments:* a range of tambourines, triangles, tongue drums, wood blocks, tambours, metal and wooden agogos, cow bells (hand held or mounted), Indian bells, small bongo drums, vibraslap, Latin American frying pan (frigideiro);
- *scraping instruments:* cabasa, afuche de coco;
- *blowing instruments:* nightingale call, quail call, instruments demanding two notes (ocarinas, toned whistles, etc);
- *pitched instruments:* soprano and alto glockenspiels, xylophones and metallophones (with the option of removing notes), individual and clusters of chime bars, individual toned hand chimes.

Upper Key stage 2/3

Instruments for this stage should include those that are big in size and more sophisticated in appearance. Pupils should be challenged with a range of instruments from different cultures that demand different skills. Introduction of these should nevertheless be phased, so that pupils are not bombarded with a bewildering range, and so that they have a chance to master particular instruments. Pupils need to be aware of a range of options on playing instruments in different ways; for example, the effect of playing with different kinds of beaters and more than one beater at the same time.

Instruments available for exploration may include all the above, in addition:

- *shaking instruments:* large rainmaker tubes, shekere, cabasas of different sizes;
- *tapping instruments:* Irish bodhran, mounted wooden temple blocks on stand, bongo drums on a stand, conga drums, Indian tabla drums, talking drums, drum kit;
- *scraping instruments:* Chinese bell tree, washboard;
- *blowing instruments:* panpipes, harmonicas, recorders, melodica;
- *pitched instruments:* kalimba (thumb piano), bass, alto and soprano metallophone and xylophone (working with white and/or black notes), keyboard, tubular bells, piano, guitar.

Using Music Technology
(by Derek Paice)

Information Technology and electronic equipment may enhance the music experience of pupils with learning difficulites in that, for example, a sophisticated musical effect can be achieved at the touch of a button:

> 4.26 ... Potentially, at least, many of those barriers to effective music making which are encountered by pupils who lack advanced traditional musical skills have been removed (NCC, 1991, p9–10).

The National Curriculum (DFE, 1995) requires for *all* pupils that:

> [They] should be given opportunities, where appropriate, to develop and apply their information technology (IT) capability in their study of music (p1).

Access to music may be enhanced by making use of *appropriate* technology. This may be said of all phases and abilities although there are special issues in relation to the education of pupils who have special needs. Music technology (a more useful term in this context than 'information technology') may be used for its functions of creating, processing, recording, replaying and enhancing sound. There has been much work in recent years on the development of a broader range of user interfaces (including switches and sensors), and when these are used the effect can be truly liberating and very exciting.

Effective use of music technology does not have to incur expenditure beyond your budget, although if you are planning to be a serious user it will obviously pay to have the 'tools of the trade'. Let us consider equipment you will already have in school and possible ways of augmenting your provision.

Recording

All schools will have access to a tape recorder of some description. A standard cassette player is such a well established part of the information storage and retrieval scene that we tend not to include it in when we think of 'information technology'. At its most basic, a cassette player can be used to record the sounds made by a pupil and to play them back. Obviously the feedback to the pupil takes place after the tape has been rewound. There are a few precautions to bear in mind when using tape recorders. In the main, you get what you pay for, but even a basic machine will give you better recordings if you bear two things in mind and both have to do with noise.

(1) *Microphone – internal*

The standard cassette player has a built in microphone. All tape recorders have parts that whirr and hum. It stands to reason that if the microphone is close to the source of the noise you do not want to hear, you'll record more of it than you need (and certainly more than you'll want). Always try to use a tape recorder with an external microphone – that is, one you have to plug into the machine. That way you will record more of the pupil and less of the tape machinery.

(2) *Microphone – external*

If you have to buy a microphone you will probably be presented with two types at the cheap end of the scale. A dynamic mic will generally cope better with loud sounds at close quarters. The more expensive dynamic mics are used professionally in live performing situations. The cheaper ones tend to manage the middle frequencies, but cannot cope with extremes of low and high frequencies. Electret condenser microphones are cheaper versions of studio condenser mics and require a battery, usually fitted into the barrel of the mic. They are more fragile, do not respond well to loud sound at close quarters and sometimes stop working if there is too much moisture present (if they are placed too close to the mouth, for example), but they do generally record a brighter, clearer signal and the microphone can be placed further away from the subject.

In the end it's up to you to compromise between what you think sounds best and how much you can afford. Don't forget that the plugs fitted to the microphone have to match the sockets on your tape recorder and for this reason as well as the ones of subjective preference already mentioned, it is usually better to take your tape recorder with you when you go to buy a microphone. Try a few out in the shop and hear the differences on your tape recorder.

Additionally, it is important to remember when recording your pupils' music that music generally has a wider frequency range than speech. If you've spent money on a microphone you can spoil your recording by using cheap tape. All recordings contain noise and although the sound is sometimes over bright for some tastes, a chrome (or 'type II') cassette will usually give clearer and cleaner results.

If you want to use your cassette recorder for special effects you could try using a telephone answering machine cassette which runs in a continual loop. Whatever you record will keep repeating and can be used as part of an interesting texture. These tapes can be bought in different lengths which run from a few seconds to a few minutes. If your machine has the facility for adjusting the speed, try playing back at a different speed from the one you recorded at.

A portastudio is a combined cassette recorder and audio mixer. It will allow you to record several layers of sound, one at a time, without necessarily erasing what you have already recorded. These start at about £300 (at time of writing).

Amplification

Whereas a tape recorder will not necessarily give instant results to the user, a microphone plugged into an amplifier and connected to a loudspeaker would. A simple way of achieving this if you don't have an amplifier and speaker is to plug a microphone into the mic input socket of the cassette unit in your hi-fi (assuming it has one), insert a cassette and switch to 'record'. By adjusting the cassette deck's input volume and the main volume control on the amplifier, you can amplify your pupil's sound as it happens. So-called karaoke are available, which combine a cassette player, amplifier and speaker in one box, with microphone inputs. If you are using your hi-fi amplifier, you could also adjust the tone and balance controls to alter the timbre and apparent origin of the sound.

Effects

Almost everything mentioned so far could be achieved with a minimal outlay. However, you can achieve some ear catching effects by plugging an effects device, such as a delay or reverb unit, between the microphone and amplifier. These devices range in size and style, from the effects pedal you might see a guitarist using on stage to sophisticated single and multi-effects units costing many hundreds of pounds. Effects units and signal processors make their changes to raw sounds by altering characteristics of the frequency (pitch), amplitude (volume) or timing of events. The range of effects available is also increasing: with some multi-effects devices, you can programme several effects together to achieve a complicated overall sound. Plugging the microphone into the input socket on the delay unit, and plugging the output of the delay unit into the amplifier input, will enable your pupils to amaze themselves with the range of echoey sounds they have made! Not particularly vocal children may suddenly find a voice when they can hear the processed results of their utterances. These effects units currently can be purchased for under £150 (education prices) although, again, you could pay much more without trying too hard.

Sound sources

So far we have only considered technology to enhance or capture sounds which the pupil can make. Apart from keyboards there are many other electronic devices for making or creating sound. If your keyboard has MIDI sockets fitted you may wish to expand the range of sounds your keyboard might produce by adding a sound module which is, in effect, another keyboard, but without the keys. MIDI can open up a world of sonic possibilities, but beware, it is fraught with frustration if you do not have the experience to trace the sources of problems which will inevitably occur. MIDI instruments may now be controlled not just by piano type keyboards but by such interfaces as pressure sensitive drum pads, wind controllers (which you blow like playing a saxophone or trumpet, for example), MIDI microphones, movement sensors and all sorts of switches. Organisations such as The Drake Music Project exist to advise and enable people with a physical disability to make music. If you begin to look at using computers the options expand still further. Computer music software is available to enable you to save your music, and later recall and edit it in great detail if required, but most usefully, however, this can happen at the pupils' own pace: they can review their music visually on screen as well as aurally.

Mixing

One piece of equipment which would make life easier once you have started using music technology to any degree would be a mixer. This, as the name suggests, is a device which allows you to take signals from more than one source (for example, several microphones and/or keyboards) and mix them together. One reason for doing this would be to enable you to record the contribution of several pupils simultaneously on your single tape recorder. The majority of mixers also allow you to adjust the level of an incoming signal you are sending to a signal processor or effects unit, which clearly offers you more control of the sound. At their most basic, a mixer will give you control over the volume levels on each channel of sound only. These simple four channel mixers can be bought for upwards of £20 (at time of going to press). To make flexible use of microphones, electronic instruments, and effects devices your mixer should really have additionally: input gain (to boost or cut an in-coming signal), e.q. (or equalisation – to enable control over tone), auxiliary (or effects) sends and returns, and pan controls (for moving sound within the stereo spectrum).

EXAMPLE
The following example illustrates a voice work session with pupils with PMLD, enhanced with music technology – Boss RDD20 Digital Delay, a domestic cassette deck, a mixer (we used a Boss BX600). Issues relating to planning music activity in relation to pupils with learning difficulties will be given full consideration in the next chapter.

Activities:	**Rationale:**
Establishing the theme: • hello song, varied with singing pupils' names, staff harmonising around the melody	ritual song; chance to focus on individuals; gaining attention; experience of listening to texture of voices
Introductory activity: • establish slow pulse using unvoiced sounds: pah – pah – pah – pah...staff all joining in and individual staff improvising rhythmically: brrr – brrrr – , chaca – chaca – pah-pah, whoo-whoo-pah ... microphone offered to pupils to capture and incorporate pupils' spontaneous breathing (laughter, guttural sounds, squeals, etc) ... gradually getting louder, then fading	group musical experience; work on pulse, rhythm, texture and dynamics amplifying the pupils' vocalisations makes the sound appear from somewhere else – ie from where the loudspeaker is situated
Development and exploration: • individual pupils to make a sound into microphone – voiced and unvoiced; these recorded and overlain, to make a tape loop of repeated sound phrases	texture – collage from individual sounds
• establish a unison drone: sustained, low sound performed by staff, then sliding sound upwards to produce a high-pitched drone; then starting high and sliding down to a low-pitched drone	awareness of pitch, extending vocal range
• microphone offered to individual pupils – staff reinforce spontaneous vocalisation by imitating it and shaping it musically into a repeated rhythmic phrase, voiced and unvoiced – eg eeya-uh eeya-uh; layering different pupils' sounds in repeated phrases	developing structure from improvised sound
• making sounds on different body parts – eg lip smacking, kissing hands squeakily, snorting, sneezing, slapping knees, slurping – using these over a vocal rhythmic pulse – aaa-ha-ha, aaa-ha-ha ; contrasting loud and soft sounds, shaping pupils' spontaneous sounds into a repeated pattern using voiced and unvoiced sounds	timbre – awareness of different qualities of sounds; texture

Activities:	**Rationale:**

Selecting towards composition:
- improvising around individual pupils' names, experimenting with different ways of vocalising syllables: long sounds, short staccato sounds, extending over a high-low vocal range; repeating as a rhythmic pattern; enhancing with echo and reverb effects; putting long and short names together, overlaying different pupils to produce a textured montage piece of unison and harmonising phrases:
Leeeee – Leeeeee – Leeeeee
Ddddd-danny Ddddd-danny
Waaaaaayne – Waaaaaayne
Donnadonnadonnadonna
- good'bye song within normal range, staff harmonising to create a Barber shop effect!

pitch; duration; texture; individual contributions given structure towards devising a group composition

switch on the delay unit and turn up the feedback control until about five or six repeats are heard

adjusting modulation depth gives the effect of the repeats changing pitch adjusting modulation rate gives a very 'other worldly' effect

focusing on individuals in ritual activity; varying familiar song to create a soothing, relaxing finish

CHAPTER 3

Planning Classroom Music

This chapter will consider guidelines for structuring a classroom music lesson which may be used as a framework for planning across the age and ability range. It will also offer procedures for evaluating and monitoring classroom music, with a view to informing future development in a module of work. Whilst lesson planning tends to be driven by the musical experiences offered to the group, material at the same time should be differentiated to meet individual pupils' needs.

Planning a Lesson

Certain factors will need to be taken into consideration when planning a lesson:

- classroom music, whilst supporting and enriching cross-curricular topic work, essentially needs to focus on pupils' progress in the musical elements, the development of their playing and aural skills;
- the lesson should be active, weighted in favour of pupils' own music-making;
- pupils should also be offered opportunities for listening to and appraising music, whether pre-recorded or their own compositions – this should be integral to the music-making process;
- there should be a balance between teacher-directed tasks and more open-ended work;
- recognition should be given to the development of individual pupils' vocal as well as instrumental skills;
- strategies should be used to access activities according to pupils' abilities, such as the use of supporting visual stimuli and multi-sensory devices to reinforce the musical content;
- teachers need to plan for exploration *in depth* of an aspect of music, rather than stringing together a succession of unrelated activities.

A music lesson will have four phases:

> **Stage 1: Establishing the theme**
> – hello song or familiar greeting activity
> – use of a stimulus (extract of music? a picture? an object? a song?)
> – introducing musical aims related to the stimulus, eg:
>   • composition work on the idea of 'the town' using Gershwin's 'American in Paris' as an initial example;
>   • sound collage involving texture and timbre based on a picture of the countryside;
>   • rhythm work taken from a song;
>   • work on duration – long smooth sounds developed from a stone stimulus, etc.
>
> **Stage 2: Introductory activities related to the theme**
> – teacher-led task to establish rapport and group dynamic
> – warm-up exercise or musical game based on the stimulus and/or associated musical element, eg:
>   • singing a song;
>   • joining in with a rhythmic group pulse;
>   • singing long open vowel sounds;
>   • repeated chant based on the theme, etc.
>
> **Stage 3: Development and exploration of the theme**
> – variable number of structured teacher-led tasks to reinforce the theme – a musical idea and/or a musical element
> – in-depth activities to challenge musical skills in playing and/or singing
> – selecting and using appropriate instruments
>
> **Stage 4: Selecting towards composition**
> – open-ended activities geared at pupils' self-expression through music
> – narrowing the pupils' focus on relevant material from which to make creative choices
> – organising and 'fixing' sounds into a structure
> – reflecting on, refining and modifying composition (individual, small group or whole group) towards sharing and performing to others
> – ritual goodbye song/activity (optional!)

Stage 1: Establishing the theme

A 'hello' song or regular greeting activity carried out ritualistically from session to session may help to focus pupils' attention and set the context for the ensuing music session. The teacher should have in mind a particular aspect on which to focus from the Music Programme of Study, which will provide the theme for the lesson. The theme may be taken from aspects of composing, performing or listening to music, and may be explored in isolation or in combination. For example:

- the teacher may consider that the group needs to focus on one particular musical element, such as tempo;
- alternatively, the emphasis may be on (for example) performing with others,

in which case the activities will be structured towards facilitating the pupils working autonomously in groups;
- pupils' attention initially may need to be captured through an appealing stimulus; for example, watching a balloon bouncing may reinforce the notion of the action required to master the use of a beater on a chime bar, as well as suggesting a structure for a composition – the balloon gently bouncing along then bursting with a sudden explosive bang.

In practice, the teacher may also have in mind an aim related to performing and composing (eg creating musical effects to illustrate a story), and at the same time an aim related to listening and appraising (eg recognising how sounds are used to achieve a particular effect). Although a particular aspect may be selected on which to focus, invariably the other musical elements will be worked on simultaneously and used in support of one another.

Additionally, the teacher will need to be aware of *individual pupils'* stages of development in different aspects of music, and how they may be challenged. The teacher will need to ensure that ensuing activities are differentiated to meet individual needs. For example, in a class group composition to illustrate a story through music, one pupil may select an appropriate instrument to represent a particular sound – such as the sea by a maraca – whilst another pupil may decide when and how contrast in dynamics should be introduced.

Stage 2: Introductory activities related to the theme

The opening activity will need to be sufficiently stimulating and motivating to gain the attention of the group. It will set the tone and context for the rest of the lesson; subsequent activities will stem from it. Therefore the activity needs to offer challenges appropriate to the age, ability and needs of the participants. In the main, this opening task will be a group activity, directly related to a stimulus or theme. It will be suitably energising according to the mood of the group; the teacher will need to be flexible in the way opening material is presented. For example, one group may need a rousing rendition of 'Old Macdonald had a Farm' in order to stimulate a creative flow of energy; the same group on another occasion (eg a windy day after playtime!) may need this delivered in a calm, quiet wistful manner.

Intrinsic to the material in this opening activity should be musical elements and aspects from the Programme of Study that offer potential for further exploration. The activity – a musical game, song or warm-up exercise – will have been selected according to the perceived musical needs of the group. It will be important that pupils are able to achieve easily in this opening activity to ensure early confidence and success and to warm up the participants. Most suitable activities, therefore, will be those with which they are already familiar, or else one with an uncomplicated structure which pupils may easily contribute to or embellish.

Stage 3: Development and exploration of the theme

The teacher will then work with the pupils through a succession (variable number) of activities, with the purpose of focusing in depth on a particular musical aspect emerging from the opening activity. The pupils will be challenged to develop work on instruments and/or using the voice. Activities need to be carefully structured by the teacher, so that the pupils are offered specific parameters in which to develop their musical skills. The emphasis will be on the development of pupils' ability to *make* music. Listening tasks as such will be used specifically to support pupils' music making, rather than used as an end in themselves.

Activities should become progressively more challenging, with a view to developing:

- the pupils' grasp of the music element(s) in question;
- their ability to play and/or sing with others;
- individual skills.

Stage 4: Selecting towards composition

From the range of material that will have been covered, the teacher will now need to isolate particular strands which will offer the pupils creative opportunities. These should be specifically related to the teacher's original intent with regard to the group's learning need. However, it is important to remain flexible to the group's interests and other learning needs that may emerge during the course of the lesson, and possibly capitalise on this creatively by harnessing the pupils' ideas. Pupils' creative input during this part of the lesson may be:

- *improvising:* spontaneously working out sound patterns within a given framework (eg on a xylophone using notes C D E G, the others having been removed);
- *composing:* shaping musical ideas to achieve an original piece of music;
- *arranging:* reworking an existing piece of music (eg devising a percussion part to accompany a familiar song).

In this part of the lesson, skills in making music will be channelled towards achieving a creative piece (whether solo, as part of a small group or within the context of the whole class). Greater emphasis perhaps will be given to listening and appraising work in progress. Pupils need to be constructively critical in order to review and modify their own and others' compositions. The pupils will need to be enabled to create with the musical elements and other relevant musical skills (such as their ability to control sound). This will have to be accessed in a way that is relevant to their ability. For example, pupils with profound and multiple learning difficulties will need considerable support to achieve a creative intention. Pupils' social skills may also affect their ability to work with others to organise and perform sounds as part of a group.

The teacher will need to be aware of differentiating the structure in which pupils are to make creative decisions; for example, one small group of pupils may be able to devise a piece to an A-B-A structure (like a musical sandwich!). Where A and B are different sections; another group may be able to compose a rondo with an A-B-A-C-A structure (a double-decker musical sandwich!). With certain groups of pupils with learning difficulties, it may be more viable to develop composition work with the whole group, with individuals (or small groupings of pupils) challenged according to their respective ability to contribute to the whole group piece. Alternatively, pupils may be able to work in small groups, with staff strategically placed in order to support sensitively, to tease out pupils' creativity – staff may need to be carefully briefed over their role, in order not to dominate or be over-directive.

In order to 'fix' the sounds and to create a structure, compositions may be notated on a score through the use of graphic or pictorial symbols, as an alternative to traditional notation. Use of a cassette recorder will enable improvised work to be instantly 'trapped' and replayed, so that pupils may rework their material. Sufficient time should be planned into the lesson, for pupils to *reflect* on and discuss their work. The teacher's comments may draw pupils' attention to particular features of the music, with a possible option of refining the work further. It may not always be appropriate to channel composition towards a formal performance, although this may enhance pupils' motivation. The aim of this part of the lesson should be enabling pupils to express themselves creatively rather than to feel the pressure of completing a finished piece. It may well be preferable to carry work over several sessions rather than finishing the teacher's lesson plan in one.

Teachers may wish to conclude a lesson with a regular 'goodbye' song or ritual activity. This can serve to bring the whole group together after working in small groups, as well as to 'frame' the session before moving on to a different activity.

Evaluating a Lesson

The following questions may help in considering the effectiveness and value of a music experience offered to pupils in any lesson:

Structuring the lesson:

- Were the activities you selected appropriate to achieve your intentions?
- Was there a balance in the kind of activities, between structured teacher-led tasks and open-ended creative work?
- Did you change direction during the lesson? Why? What effect did this have?
- Was there sufficient opportunity for pupils to make music – individually and/or as part of a group, to listen to and talk about music?

Responding to developments:

- Was the group sufficiently enabled to explore an aspect of music in depth?
- Were your comments appropriate and enabling? How did they affect the pupils' work?
- What ideas or signals did the pupils initiate? How did you respond? Did you compromise or miss any creative opportunities?
- Were the pupils sufficiently enabled to create original work at their respective levels of ability?
- Was the choice of material and available instruments appropriate for the pupils' stage of development?

Date............................... **MUSIC LESSON PLAN** Group............................
Time............................... Staff..............................
National Curriculum refs................................ ....
Resources required...

ESTABLISHING THE THEME
What musical aims will the lesson address? (eg composition work? musical elements? aspects of listening?) Will I use a stimulus? (extract of music? a picture? an object? a song?) How will I set up the room? How will I organise resources?

↓

INTRODUCTORY ACTIVITIES
Teacher-led task to establish rapport and group dynamic. Warm-up exercises and musical games based on the stimulus and/or associated musical element(s).

↓

DEVELOPMENT AND EXPLORATION
Variable number of structured teacher-led tasks to reinforce the theme. In-depth activities to challenge musical skills in playing and/or singing. Selecting and using appropriate instruments.

↓

SELECTING TOWARDS COMPOSITION
Open-ended activities. Focusing on relevant material from which to make creative choices. Organising and 'fixing' sounds into a structure. Reflecting, refining and modifying composition (individual/small groups/whole group?) towards presenting to others.

EVALUATION – Commments and Future Priorities

The teaching context:

- Did you maximise the resource of supporting staff?
- What extraneous pressures shaped the lesson? Time? Pace? Space? Interruptions? Noise thresholds?
- Did anything unexpected arise during the lesson? How did you respond?
- What was the attitude of the pupils? How did they affect you? Did they change?

Teaching decisions:

- Did you communicate instructions clearly or was there confusion?
- Did the activities contain the pupils and keep them suitably focused and on task?
- Were activities and tasks sufficiently differentiated to meet the needs of all the pupils?
- Did all the pupils demonstrate their achievements?
- How did you set up activities? By requests? Choices? Orders? Negotiation? Did you feel comfortable with this?

Each of the following chapters (4, 5 and 6) features a recording sheet to assist in monitoring an individual pupil's progress in making, composing and listening to music respectively. They offer a means for noting an individual pupil's progress over six separate occasions; for example, these could be once a week over a half-term, or once every half-term over a school year. A grading system from 1 to 6 is suggested, of individual progress towards achieving long-term goals in all the different aspects of music activity (see chapters 4, 5 and 6). Grading is intended to refer to sub-stages achieved – shorter-term objectives – for each of these areas, according to criteria identified in chapters 4, 5 and 6. In all cases, teachers' supporting comments will be crucial, in order to indicate the basis – the evidence – on which assessments are made of pupils' responses and achievements. Also to indicate future learning needs for pupils.

EXAMPLES OF CLASSROOM MUSIC LESSONS

Lower Key stage 1 (including nursery/reception/pupils with PMLD)

topic: 'myself' – body awareness
music themes: the element of tempo – contrasts between slow/sustained and fast; also responding to the mood of a piece of music
stimulus: tape of 'Hens and Cocks' from Saint-Saëns' 'Carnival of the Animals' (distinct contrasting slow then fast sections)
resources: lengths of thick knicker elastic with hand loops oversewn; whirly tubes of alternating colours, connected by a long length of very thick knicker or trampoline elastic
instruments: handled and wrist bells – in order not to impede movement, nor drown out taped accompaniment

Activities:	Rationale:
establishing the theme:	
• 'hello' song, varied with singing pupils' names through a whirly tube	establish group rapport; chance to focus on individuals; gaining attention
• using whirly tube to demonstrate fast and slow movement with accompanying sounds	introducing stimulus and musical theme for the lesson
introductory activity:	
• action song, everyone sitting in circle, supported by staff as required, holding on to whirlies linked by thick elastic: 'here we go side to side to side, side to side forwards and backwards, forwards and backwards up and down, up and down and here we go again ...' Repeat song three times, getting faster each time, finishing last verse with '... now we're going to STOP'	consolidating the group; reinforcing theme of tempo performing a song as a whole group experience elastic to reinforce experience of sustained tension in relation to others
development and exploration:	
• holding on to whirlies as whole group, raising arms slowly then fast to accompanying tape of 'Hens and Cocks'	generalising concept of slow/fast contrast in relation to another piece of music understanding a piece of music through active listening (making a physical response)
• replacing elastic with small hand-held percussion, and playing along to accompanying tape of 'Hens and Cocks', slow then fast	transferring concept of fast/slow actions into making music
• individual turn-taking activity, accompanied by 'Hens and Cocks' each time: individual pupil to have length of elastic looped over opposite hand/	reinforcing response to contrasting tempo in a heard piece of music – positive or negative reaction to different speeds?

Activities:	**Rationale:**
foot, with limbs manipulated by staff ... then quickly lifted on to blanket and slid rapidly round the floor for duration of second fast section of the music, returning to original place as the piece reaches its climax.	experience of stretching in response to slow sustained section of the music experiencing contrast of fast music

selecting towards composition:

● pupils to select hand-held percussion from choice structured by the teacher (eg bells or small shaker)	exploring possible range of sounds of their own choice; indicating preferences
● conductor (staff and/or pupil) to control the group, by indicating alternating slow then fast playing, staff supporting pupils as necessary	performing with others within clear boundaries
● conductor to indicate solo slow playing then fast ensemble playing – record on tape	exploring possible variations with structure
● re-play tape immediately to the pupils – reactions?	communicating/expressing their feelings in response to their own work
● 'goodbye' song	familiar routine song to close the lesson

future developments:
● using the tape of fast/slow music for movement work
● repeating the lesson with different percussion – exploring fast/slow using different sounds
● responding to different pieces of music from other cultures and times, with distinct fast/slow sections
● singing familiar songs fast/slow

Upper Key stage 1

topic: animals
music themes: the element of dynamics – extremes of loud and soft; also how sounds are used for effect
stimulus: 'Worms Wiggle' – children's pop-up book; children to select *one* animal, and think of two contrasting actions to reflect the way that animal moves to make up a three part story about that animal to be expressed musically – eg A-B-A-B-A (a repeated two-part musical pattern) for the lion stalking then roaring then stalking; tape of the 'Lion March' from Saint-Saëns' 'Carnival of the Animals'
resources: felt board; pictures of animals performing contrasting actions (eg a lion stalking and a lion roaring); cuddly (eg lion) toy
instruments: small hand-held percussion which can be shaken or rattled to create the effect of a lion roaring

Activities:	**Rationale:**
establishing the theme:	
● familiar 'hello' song	establishing group; chance to focus on individuals; opportunity for pupil choice; gaining attention
● read action story of 'Worms Wiggle' – focus on the lion stalking – what else does the lion do? (roar!)	
introductory activity:	
● play game around the circle, cuddly toy is passed around; the person left holding it when the verse stops has to say their name either loudly or softly: 'Round and round the circle, Round and round the circle Round and round the circle Until the music stops'	introducing concepts of loud/soft; teaching skills in turn-taking for group work
development and exploration:	
● show picture of lion roaring – pupils to make a loud sound with the voice; contrast with a quiet sound (eg unvoiced p-p-p-p-) to match the picture of the lion stalking	working on extremes of dynamics
● repeat the lion roaring, this time starting quietly and getting louder	challenging pupils towards gradation of volume
● hand out percussion – everyone to play on clear cue from conductor (makaton sign for 'play') and stop on cue of conductor's hands together	establishing clear start/stop signals – the conductor as the controller of the group's music-making
● conductor to hold up picture of lion stalking for everyone to play quietly; conductor to hold up picture of lion roaring – everyone to play loudly	

Activities:	**Rationale:**
• conductor (child or adult) to alternate picture prompts for loud/quiet playing	sequencing contrasts of sounds via the conductor

selecting towards composition:

• teacher-led composition, about a story of a lion who wakes up, stalks on his way through the jungle, roars at the other lions and goes on his way again: lion waking – pupils pick up their instruments lion stalking – pupils play quietly lion roaring – pupils play loudly lion stalking – pupils play quietly	using a simple story line as a basic structure
• 'score' composition by 'fixing' it using picture prompts on the felt board	use of pictorial images to relate sound to symbol
• conductor to indicate 'play' and point to pictures in sequence, then indicate 'stop' with hands together	conductor deciding lengths of the sections
• record composition on tape – play back immediately and consider refinements (eg starting the roar quietly and getting louder) – repeat	
• listen to the 'Lion March' from Saint-Saëns' 'Carnival of the Animals' – can they hear the lion roaring?	active listening – relating different ways to create the sounds of the lion (orchestral string instruments)

future developments:
- use dynamics to express different ideas – eg storm/calm
- use other animals from 'Worms Wiggle' as a basis for structuring simple composition around two contrasting actions expressed musically, or a simple story line (eg seagull gliding, pecks at a fish then glides off again)
- use the pupils' composition and/or Saint-Saëns' version on tape as accompaniment for dance work – for the pupils to respond to music through movement

Lower Key stage 2

topic: the seasons – winter
musical themes: the elements of timbre and texture; also how sounds are used for effect
resources: Vaughan Williams' 'Sinfonia Antarctica' – opening extract; 'Winter' from Vivaldi's 'The Seasons'; large sheet of paper and coloured marker pens
stimulus: large poster/picture/photograph/painting of a winter landscape;
instruments: metal instruments that are cold to the touch; small percussion that can 'shiver'; hard beaters to produce a crisp sound; small chime bars and glockenspiels to produce high tinkly sounds

Activities:

establishing the theme:
- 'hello' song
- listen to extract from 'Antarctica' – does it remind them of anything? What kind of a place?
- present picture of a cold wintery scene – reactions/responses? Channel discussion towards consideration of elements in the picture and the weather
- pass around an ice cube to consolidate the feeling of *cold!*

introductory activity:
- pretending we're feeling cold – play 'follow-my-leader' activity to warm ourselves up: rhythmic tapping/slapping on different parts of the body

development and exploration:
- place selection of metal instruments in the centre of the circle – pupil in turn to come up and choose, framed by a song – pupil to play for everyone to listen to the sound:
'Here comes Peter full of fun, I wonder what he'll do'
Here comes Peter full of fun, I wonder what he'll choose?'
- everyone to play and stop on cue from conductor (hands open/hands together) – eg to make a shivering sound to match the picture
- repeat, this time conductor bringing in individual players

Rationale:

focusing the group
responding to the mood of a piece of music;
communicating feelings and ideas

focusing group attention for expressing an idea through music

consolidating the group response; watching the leader in preparation for focusing on a conductor

structured choice – limiting availability to teach about the quality of metal sounds; introducing less familiar/more complex instruments other than basic classroom percussion – eg double agogo, cabasa, etc

establishing principles for playing as part of a group

texture – solo/ensemble playing

Activities:	Rationale:
• sort instruments into sounds that go on and on (eg large triangle, cymbal, etc), those that have short crisp sounds (eg double agogo, cowbell, metal shaker), those that go up and down (glocks, chimes)	structured work on timbre

selecting towards composition:

• re-group pupils so that they are sitting with 'like' sounds. Decide what their sounds could represent in the winter picture – eg glocks and chimes for winter stream; short sounds for icicles dripping; longer sounds for snow falling	timbre – how sounds can be used for effect according to their qualities
• pupils to work out additional sounds/instruments as required – eg cowbell for duck pecking at frozen pond	
• conductor (pupil or teacher) to bring in groups or solo players, starting and stopping on cue – record on tape	
• play back immediately, pausing after each new entry and assigning a graphic symbol (eg writing pattern on a card – lllll lllll, wwww) to each one	relating sound to graphic symbol
• re-play the tape, pausing to place the cards in order of entry on a board or large sheet, to create a graphic score	'fixing' improvisation into a structure
• repeat the composition, this time working from the score as prompted by the conductor – record on tape	modifying work
• replay immediately – reactions? Refinements? (eg should any bits be louder/quieter, etc?). Add to the score	

future developments:
- make a sound collage composition to match a different landscape – eg woodland, desert, seaside
- use selected chime bars to create ostinato pattern to represent aspects in a picture, eg slow-moving floating ice
- listen to the way other composers have portrayed winter – eg Vivaldi's 'Winter' from 'The Seasons'
- spontaneous finger painting to music – fingers walking through cold wet landscape
- repeating the lesson for warm sounds using wooden instruments, low mellow sounds using voice and/or bass percussion, to reflect Summer

Upper Key stage 2/3

topic: the rain forest – environmental awareness
musical themes: the elements of timbre, texture and duration; also how sounds are used for effect, and how sounds are made
resources: separate pictures of animals; tape of individual rain forest creatures (eg on a sound effects tape); environmental pictures to illustrate the destruction of the rain forest habitat
stimulus: poster of the rain forest
instruments: wooden percussion; ethnic instruments – shekere, tongue or slit drum, bongo drums, afuche, cabasa, guiro, etc; large skin drum on a stand and crash cymbal

Activities:	**Rationale:**
establishing the theme:	
• warm-up rhythmic name game: clap-clap-fill in name	establishing individual contribution as part of the whole group
• present poster of the rain forest – what creatures live there?	
• vary warm-up game with filling in name of a jungle creature	
introductory activity:	
• listen to isolated sounds of the rain forest on tape	timbre – identifying sounds
• imitating sounds in the rain forest using the voice – eg monkey call, tiger roar, birds, elephant trumpet	aural perception exercise
development and exploration:	
• look at pictures of environmental destruction – discuss implications: shape into a story about creatures thriving in harmony – trees being chopped down – the aftermath, to be the basis for a group composition to express their ideas	introducing notion of expressing an idea in music to communicate to others
• listen to rain forest tape again – pupils to select appropriate instruments to emulate the different sounds – solo/small groups of like instruments	timbre – matching heard sounds to instruments
selecting and towards composition:	
• shape solo/small group playing into rhythmic ostinatos – score parts on large sheet of paper, using graphic symbols (eg writing patterns) or possibly traditional notation	developing unison playing – noting rhythmic sound patterns
• identify a soloist for the middle section to represent the trees being felled, using drum roll and crash on cymbal (repeated several times)	texture – distinguishing solo/ensemble playing

Activities:	**Rationale:**

- group to decide the final section: happy ending (creatures gradually return and the rain forest regenerates?) or sad ending (total silence)
- rehearse whole piece – record on tape and play back immediately – group to consider how to improve it (eg use of dynamics, tempo, etc)
- add graphic symbols on score to indicate pitch, dynamics, tempo, density of sounds (texure – number of players), rests for moments of silence.

refining and modifying for effect – 'fixing' musical ideas

future developments:
- using pupils' composition on tape as accompaniment for dance – communicating feelings and ideas through movement to music
- refining composition into a polished performance to an audience
- developing the same theme using voices to create a sound collage to express the destruction of the rain forest
- devising a new composition based on a different environmental issue – eg pollution of the sea
- developing rhythmic ostinato on unpitched percussion into ostinato on pitched instruments
- compositions requiring players to sustain their part in unison in group music-making (keeping in time)
- listening to protest music by other artists (eg Sting, Bob Dylan, Joan Baez) on environmental and political issues

CHAPTER 4

Building Blocks – The Elements for Music-making

This chapter will look at the fundamental elements with which music can be created. Each of these elements will be considered separately, with aims and objectives taking account of and illustrated with examples of activities:

- *timbre:* quality of sound, differences between sounds;
- *texture:* one sound/several sounds, different ways of putting sounds together;
- *duration:* long/short sounds, pulse, rhythm;
- *silence:* stillness between sounds;
- *dynamics:* loud/quiet, different levels of volume;
- *tempo:* fast/slow, gradations of speed;
- *pitch:* high/low sounds, gradations of sound, chords.

These elements are interrelated in any music activity. However, for the sake of targeting a specific aspect, it is helpful to isolate the strands. It is possible to use the same music activity, therefore, on different occasions with a different agenda. For example: an activity using a cymbal could be used to reinforce awareness of length of sound; the same activity on a different occasion may be used to teach control to produce loud and soft sounds.

Examples of activities will indicate a progression within each of the elements, equivalent to a developmental curriculum through Key stages 1 and 2/3. In line with National Curriculum recommendations (DFE, 1995), teachers should select material across the Key stages, according to the developmental needs of pupils, and adapt the sophistication of content where necessary to ensure that it is age-appropriate.

The figure summarises development in the elements of music across the Key stages. These have been further sub-divided to clarify four distinct stages of development. They have also been described as 'reactive', 'active', 'interactive' and 'proactive'. To reflect broad characteristics in music work at those respective stages.

BUILDING BLOCKS
Development in the Elements of Music

Lower Key Stage 1: **Reactive**

awareness and spontaneous responses to the musical elements
- *timbre*: awareness and recognition of different sound qualities
- *texture*: discovering contrasts in solo/ensemble singing and playing
- *duration*: awareness of long/short sounds
- *silence*: awareness of breaks in sound
- *dynamics*: awareness of contrasts in sound levels (loud, quiet)
- *tempo*: awareness of contrasts in pace and speed (fast, slow)
- *pitch*: awareness of extremes in high/low sounds

Upper Key Stage 1: **Active**

development of control over and basic understanding of the elements of music
- *timbre*: widening awareness of similarities and differences in sound qualities
- *texture*: understanding solo/ensemble distinction in singing and playing
- *duration*: active control and recognition of long and short sounds
- *silence*: developing control over stillness in singing and playing
- *dynamics*: developing control over contrasts in loud/quiet playing and singing
- *tempo*: developing control over contrasts in fast/slow playing and singing
- *pitch*: understanding and recognising differences in high/low singing and playing

Lower Key Stage 2: **Interactive**

developing greater subtlety and complexity of control over the musical elements
- *timbre*: sorting more challenging and inventive sounds
- *texture*: more complex layering of sound
- *duration*: development of more complex rhythmic awareness
- *silence*: maintaining control over stillness in singing and playing with peers
- *dynamics*: developing control over gradations of volume
- *tempo*: developing control over gradations of speed
- *pitch*: discriminating more subtle distinctions over a range of high and low sounds

Upper Key Stage 2/3: **Proactive**

using the elements of music to express ideas, thoughts and feelings
- *timbre*: using sound quality for effect
- *texture*: combining sounds to achieve a particular intensity
- *duration*: using rhythmic patterns of a required length for effect
- *silence*: using silence expressively and to give structure
- *dynamics*: using a range of sound levels to give evocative quality to music
- *tempo*: using a variety of speeds in singing and playing to give expressive quality
- *pitch*: changing levels in high/low sounds to give expression and lyrical quality

Figure 4.1

Timbre

Timbre is the raw state of sound, and its differing *qualities*; for example everybody's voice will sound different, even if they are saying the same thing. It is this that is given shape when music is created. Pupils need to develop an awareness of the effects of different kinds of sounds, to be able to organise and discriminate between sounds for their evocative and expressive quality.

> *Long-term aim:*
> To select and organise sounds according to their quality to achieve a particular effect.
>
> *Short-term objectives:*
> 1. Shows awareness of a distinct sound played by the teacher; eg turns towards a clear drum beat.
> 2. Recognises sounds with a marked difference; eg identifies the sound of (eg) hoover, triangle, piano, teacher's voice, doorbell, etc.
> 3. Associates a sound maker with its output; eg chooses an instrument to play from a contrasting selection in order to produce a particular kind of sound – drum, triangle, maraca, guiro, duck call, etc.
> 4. Is aware of a range of possible ways to produce sound; eg is able to produce three different sounds from an instrument that offers versatility in playing, such as a tambourine or cymbal.
> 5. Is able to produce sounds demonstrating subtlety and versatility on a visual cue; eg alters playing to follow a conductor's lead.
> 6. Is able to control sounds sensitively to express a particular idea, mood or emotion independently in music; eg child improvises a simple story on instrument(s) that involves some peak of excitement and calm.

Lower Key stage 1 (including nursery/reception/pupils with PMLD)

- Awareness of sound: is there a sound? Where is the sound coming from?
- Turning to locate sound, responding to their name (eg in greeting song).
- Looking for a hidden noise-maker.
- Tracking a noise-maker to right, left, up, down, behind, across mid-line (using eyes? turning whole head/body).
- Recording voices of familiar people and the children's own vocal sounds – recognition?
- Different people saying the same thing: eg child's name, 'hello', etc.
- Using body as a sound source (clapping, stamping, rubbing, etc).
- Enhancing vocalisation using microphones and music technology.
- Discovering sounds in the classroom: tapping radiators, the floor, chairs, etc.
- Performing the same action on different surfaces: eg tapping the table, the carpet, chair, etc.
- Listening to pre-recorded everyday sounds: toilet flushing, doorbell, telephone, etc – response? recognition?
- Discovering sounds in the environment: eg the wind, birds, traffic, aircraft, echoes, etc.
- Playing simple percussion to create a sound: exploring tuned and untuned instruments.

Upper Key stage 1

Continue developing the above, in addition:

- Matching sounds played behind a screen: identifying the identical instrument from a limited selection on a table.
- Recording children's voices saying the same thing.
- Group voice work: focus on quality of sound, eg hissing, brr, lah – speech sounds.
- Sound lotto game: matching picture of sound source to everyday sounds on tape.

Lower Key stage 2

Continue developing the above, in addition:

- Grouping instruments that make similar sounds: eg metal, wooden, blowing, shaking, etc.
- Matching unfamiliar sounds: eg unusual instruments or objects, picture of the sound source.
- Songs to encourage versatility in playing: eg 'hot potato pass it on (repeat 3 times), get rid of the hot potato' – instrument is passed round the circle, child left holding the instrument has to find a way to play it.
- Matching two familiar instruments being played at the same time (behind a screen), identical partners on table.

Upper Key stage 2/3

Continue developing the above, in addition:

- Experimenting with the voice to produce sounds beyond its normal range – link with imagery as appropriate.
- Selecting an instrument to represent a sound in a picture: eg rhythmic ostinato performed on a rasp for a frog croaking.
- Experimenting with electronic and acoustic music: synthesised and unplugged.
- Watching a silent movie or cartoon: providing their own accompaniment using different percussion to achieve a particular effect.

Texture

Texture is the density of sound, which may be from a simple solo source or complex multiple sources. Texture is concerned with *layers of sound* and also *how* sounds are put together – options on when and how to play. Pupils need to be made aware of possibilities for combining different sounds to achieve particular effects.

> *Long-term aim:*
> To combine sounds in different ways to achieve a desired intensity.
>
> *Short-term objectives:*
> 1. Reacts to a contrast in the density of sound; eg shows awareness of a change from solo to ensemble playing or singing.
> 2. Sustains playing or singing in order to contribute to group music-making that involves solo/ensemble contrasts; eg accompanies teacher's playing or singing on small percussion.
> 3. Maintains part in a small group in a teacher-led class improvisation, starting and stopping on cue, to achieve the effect of layering different sounds; eg sustains drumming in a group of two or three, to contrast and/or combine with groups of metal instruments and/or shakers, with varied numbers of players in each group.
> 4. Demonstrates knowledge/awareness of the effect of combining different types of sounds; eg controls class music-making by conducting groups of players, to achieve an improvised piece involving different combinations of sounds.
> 5. Reflects an idea in music using different combinations of sounds; eg selects single or groups of instruments to represent images in a picture or events in a story.
> 6. Understands how sounds may be combined to achieve a desired effect, through matching sounds to symbol on a score; eg relates to single and/or broken lines to indicate drone or unison playing required from different groups of instruments, in order to create a soundscape.

Lower Key stage 1 (including nursery/reception/pupils with PMLD)

- 'Follow-my-leader' games: one pupil makes a body sound (eg clapping, stamping), everyone copies.
- Pupil chooses an instrument of which several are available (eg shakers, bells, rhythm sticks), and everyone else joins in.
- Copy-cat songs, eg 'Everybody do this', involving one person making a sound then everyone making sounds together.
- Recording pupil's vocalisation: use electronic effects such as reverb or delay, sound loops and multi-track recorder to augment the sound.

Upper Key stage 1

Continue developing the above, in addition:

- Teacher to accompany a pupil's singing or playing: percussion, guitar, piano, keyboard, chromaharp.
- Using colours to reinforce idea of building up a 'picture' of sound: eg one colour – one sound, many colours – many sounds.
- Telling a story using instruments to illustrate, where sounds gradually accumulate (relate to picture prompts, eg images on a felt board): eg owl woke up ... mouse woke up ... cat woke up ... etc.
- Pupils to have opportunities to participate in large numbers:
  – singing (whole school)
  – singing or playing instruments in their class group

– singing or playing solo (eg in musical repartee, such as 'hello' song).
- Listening for simple changes in the music on a prerecorded extract on tape: eg when voice joins accompaniment.

Lower Key stage 2

Continue developing the above, in addition:

- Solo verse and chorus singing: eg teacher sings verse and pupils join in chorus.
- Teacher organises different permutations of groupings: eg two pupils playing short sounds on claves, three pupils play a long sound on bells.
- Building sounds, maybe inspired by a picture: eg small groups of two or three pupils representing different jungle animals, using voice or percussion.
- Graphic scoring, using picture cues to represent sounds.
- Group chants, eg breakfast cereals – split class into two groups, each following a particular chant (adult to support each half): eg <u>corn-flakes/weet-a-bix.</u>

Upper Key stage 2/3

Continue developing the above, in addition:

- Using graphic notation to devise a simple score, using writing pattern symbols to represent different sounds – pupil to maintain a simple part.
- Possible introduction of some traditional notation.
- Use of the drone to develop simple harmony, building up chords using drones of different pitches.
- Using pitched instruments (one and two-handed playing) combined with drum beat to layer repeated patterns.

Duration

Duration is concerned with the *length* of a single sound, which may be sustained or short (eg cymbal compared to wood block). A steady repeated single sound whether played or sensed is the *pulse* or beat of the music. Long and short sounds combined in a repeated pattern make *rhythm*. Pupils need to develop their innate response to a pulse, and have this extended with increasingly challenging rhythmic patterns.

Lower Key stage 1 (including nursery/reception/pupils with PMLD)

- Making resonant sounds using cymbals, bells, gongs, etc, and long vocal sounds made by supporting staff, eg hissing, humming, wordless singing.
- Physically able pupils may make long sounds (using instruments, voice or body sounds) for the teacher to 'move' to the sound: eg in role as life-size puppet who comes to life.
- Using quieter small percussion to encourage awareness of short sounds: eg claves, small tambour, wood blocks, xylophone; teacher may reinforce

> *Long-term aim:*
> To maintain a rhythmic pattern for a required length of time.
>
> *Short-term objectives:*
> 1. Shows awareness of extremes of long and short sounds, through exploratory playing on instruments; eg reacts to stimulus of a long sound on a cymbal followed by short playing on claves.
> 2. Makes an innate physical response to a strong rhythmic pulse; eg sways to waltz music on tape, stamps feet to 'Grand Old Duke of York' march, etc.
> 3. Exerts conscious control to produce a series of sounds of a particular length; eg maintains a steady beat on simple percussion to accompany a familiar song.
> 4. Adapts playing to keep in time with an imposed pulse at different speeds; eg teacher sets keyboard beat (or metronome or drum) for pupil to accompany on percussion, with variations in the tempo.
> 5. Adapts playing to maintain a steady beat, alternating long and short sounds in a repeated pattern; eg a strong slow pulse followed by quiet quick pulse in a repeated simple pattern.
> 6. Sustains a rhythmic pattern of a fixed length in solo or ensemble playing, stopping on cue from a conductor or graphic score; eg associates sound with symbol by following a graphic pattern – lili lili lili lili.

awareness of the sound of each instrument by imitating vocally (eg clicking tongue).

- Contrasting sounds in juxtaposition to encourage greater awareness: short sounds – long sounds – short sounds. Response? Preference?
- Steady beat, moving rhythmically to musical accompaniment: clapping, stamping, swaying; aim to fade out support, so that the pupil responds independently and spontaneously.
- Pupil to beat with hand (on floor, tambourine or drum) to his or her natural pulse, teacher to join in with the pupil, gradually introducing a change in the pulse – can the pupil stop when the teacher stops?
- Rhythmic chanting (by staff) of pupils' names.
- Developing a pupils' utterance into a pulsating phrase using sound equipment for mixing and amplification.
- Responding to contrasting rhythms in juxtaposition: eg jerky – smooth – jerky.
- Opportunities to have access to large playing surfaces, eg large gong, large tympani, to develop control from the shoulder to produce sounds of different lengths.

Upper Key stage 1

Continue developing the above, in addition:

- Using a variety of unpitched instruments (eg wood-block, small tambour, maraca, etc) that demand simple motoric control and which present contrasting lengths of sound (eg maraca – long, wood-block – short).
- Use of large cymbal: pupil to 'damp', so exerting control over the length of the sound.

- Teacher plays instrument or taped music, children to accompany on simple percussion: teacher varies length of their playing through obvious contrasts of long and short sections.
- Using the voice to make long open vowel sounds (eg 'oooooh'); contrast with short staccato sounds of consonants (eg ' t-t-t-t-t-t-t-t').
- Listening and moving spontaneously and independently to rhythmic music: eg rocking, swaying, stopping when the music stops.
- Using body sounds to accompany music: eg clap, stamp, click fingers.
- Using slow pulse beats and fast ones: eg 'Humpty Dumpty' played/sung slowly then fast – pupils to accompany using body sounds or simple instruments to maintain a steady beat.
- Using songs/familiar tunes with strong rhythmic element: eg 'Hot Cross Buns' (1-2-3 rhythm repeats), to foster control over a steady pulse.
- Pupil to exert conscious control of length of an utterance (eg name or speech sound) made into a microphone; teacher may use music technology to enhance the sound, effectively 'playing about' to vary the length of the sound produced (eg echoing the pupil's name).

Lower Key stage 2

Continue developing the above, in addition:

- Grouping instruments which make obvious short sounds (eg claves, tambour, wood-block) and long sounds (eg cymbal, gong, large triangle, vibraslap).
- Pupil to 'conduct' group playing: hands open to play, hands together to indicate stop, the conductor varying the length of playing.
- Using a visual stimulus (eg spinning top, bubbles, rolling ball, bouncing balloon, puppet dancing): play when the stimulus moves, stop when it comes to rest.
- Awareness of continuous background sounds in the immediate environment, eg fluorescent lights humming, central heating, traffic, the wind.
- Building up a soundscape to go with a scene in a picture (eg seaside, busy street, countryside); incorporate long and short sounds: eg sea as on-going long sound (using maracas or voices) with intermittent shorter sounds (eg seagulls made by voices).
- Clapping or beating to songs and musical accompaniment with varied rhythmic element: 2/4 (a march), 3/4 (a waltz).
- Maintaining a steady beat led by the teacher, or by a pupil.
- Clapping syllables to pupils' names – guess whose name from a clapped rhythm only.
- Pupil to imitate short simple rhythmic phrase clapped or played by the teacher.

Upper Key stage 2/3

Continue developing the above, in addition:

- Using more sophisticated, exotic, fragile and complex percussion instruments to make long and short sounds: eg on shekere, afuche, agogo bells, keyboard etc.

- Distinguishing between staccato playing (short, sharp) and legato (long, smooth).
- Using a mixture of instruments with varying resonance: pupils to play their instrument when the previous one has stopped reverberating.
- Developing more controlled playing towards introducing notation (graphically or basic traditional – crotchets, quavers, minims).
- Having one minute's silence (what can you hear?) or work from a picture of a scene: considering sounds that are background or foreground (continuous or intermittent), and selecting instruments to represent these sounds to make a group composition.
- Establishing a pulse beat (eg slapping knees), then playing 'switch': change the pulse by using a different body part (eg clapping hands), making the beat faster or slower.
- Rhythmic playing to accompany familiar songs and tunes (eg 'Baa Baa Black Sheep'): can they recall the rhythm without the accompaniment?
- Using a keyboard to select different rhythms, pupils to join in clapping or beating along: march, waltz, rhumba, etc, work towards accompanying more syncopated irregular rhythm.
- Playing 'magic numbers': clap on a specific number, eg 1-2-3-<u>4</u> (clap on 4) – 1-2-3-<u>4</u> (clap on 4) – 1-2-3-<u>4</u>- (clap on 4) and so on, to establish a repeated pattern.
- Composing a simple piece of long/short sounds; introduce traditional notation as a way of representing the length of the sounds (crotchets, quavers) – groups could perform to each other, swapping over their scores.

Silence

Silence is the space between sounds, and provides a 'frame' for any piece of music. In music, the silence between sounds is called a 'rest', which may be of varying lengths. This implies a degree of control over the sound source (whether instrument or voice), which needs to be achieved. Silence may need to be explicitly taught to many pupils with learning difficulties. For this reason, we have distinguished it as a distinct musical element, rather than subsumed it under 'dynamics' (as in the National Curriculum, DFE, 1995) or as an aspect of 'duration'.

Lower Key stage 1 (including nursery/reception/pupils with PMLD)

- Using songs and movement that involve ebb and flow, to emphasise the contrast of silence between phrases: eg 'we are rocking, we are rocking, we are rocking, now we STOP'. All action and sound freezes on 'stop' to create an intense silence.
- Playing simple percussion to accompany songs that teach go-stop-go-stop (and so on): eg 'Everybody, everybody, everybody play together, everybody, everybody STOP ... everybody, everybody, everybody play together, everybody, everybody, everybody STOP'.
- Using loud sounds to intrude into peaceful moments, to make pupils aware of the contrast: eg using a Jack-in-the-box.

> *Long-term aim:*
> Awareness of the importance of maintaining total quiet for a required length of time, to give structure to a piece of music.
>
> *Short-term objectives:*
> 1. Responds to a break in a sound source; eg ceases innate rocking or clapping, turns towards direction of absent sound, etc.
> 2. Exerts conscious control to silence an instrument or stop singing, when accompanying music is paused (cassette tape or teacher playing guitar or piano).
> 3. Freezes sound on cue, to intersperse music-making with silence/pauses; eg follows a conductor's clearly contrasting signs: hands apart (play), hands together (stop).
> 4. Maintains silence until directed to play by a conductor; eg keeps instrument still and silent whilst others play during group music-making.
> 5. Anticipates and maintains silence occurring at regular intervals during repeated rhythmic playing led by a conductor; eg joins in with simple rhythm involving rests: play-play-*stop* play-play-*stop* play-play-*stop*.
> 6. Follows a repeated rhythmic pattern including rests notated on a score; eg matches silence to a symbol representing a pause on a score, to achieve a break in the music: – – – / – – – / – – – / – – – /

Upper Key stage 1

Continue developing the above, in addition:

- Pupils to learn to pick up instruments and put them down in a controlled fashion, without making unnecessary noise.
- Pupils to stop playing when accompaniment stops.
- Listening for quiet sounds: eg pin dropping.
- Playing 'musical bumps', recognising silence: sit down when music stops.

Lower Key stage 2

Continue developing the above, in addition:

- Pupils to play instruments in appropriate and controlled way during group music activity, stopping at the end of their turn, and keeping instruments still and silent.
- Pupils to maintain silence whilst others play, taking cue to start and stop from a 'conductor' (teacher or pupil).
- Playing 'musical statues' and 'dead lions' (recognition of silence and stillness).
- Filling a silence with a musical response: eg clap-clap-(say name), clap-clap (say name), etc.

Upper Key stage 2/3

Continue developing the above, in addition:

- Playing games involving counting patterns with a 'rest' (moment of silence):

eg everyone counts 1-2-3-(silent on 4) – 1-2-3-(silent on 4), and so on. Vary the pattern by teacher or pupil selecting a different number on which to be silent.

- Developing an ability to count inside head: eg silent (or mouthed) counting to 8, everybody do action (eg stand up) or make a single sound (eg clapping or beating) on the eighth count.
- Notating silence on a score (graphically or using traditional notation) to indicate a 'rest' (NB which really means 'get ready to play again'!).
- Playing scored compositions that include rests (maybe those devised by other groups).

Dynamics

Dynamics is concerned with *sound levels*. It can be affected by the numbers of players and which instruments are involved. Use of the full range of dynamics demands considerable control, which pupils need to acquire. Selective use of dynamics will contribute to the evocative quality of a piece of music; pupils need to be enabled to develop skills for expressing ideas, feelings and moods.

> *Long-term aim:*
> To exert appropriate energy levels to communicate an evocative quality in the music.
>
> *Short-term objectives:*
> 1. Shows awareness of extremes in dynamics; eg responds to contrasting loud/soft playing or singing by teacher and supporting staff.
> 2. Exerts conscious control to match playing to accompaniment with a marked dynamic; eg plays loudly to rousing march (live or on tape), quietly to a lullaby.
> 3. Contrasts loud and quiet playing on distinct cue from a conductor; eg matches playing to Rebus reading/communication symbols for loud (trumpet blaring) and quiet (feather).
> 4. Achieves gradation of volume to create a crescendo; eg adjusts playing or singing gradually to get louder on cue from a conductor.
> 5. Achieves gradation of volume to create a diminuendo; eg adjusts playing or singing gradually to get quieter on cue from a conductor.
> 6. Copes with sudden and/or gradual changes in loud/soft playing or singing, following visual cues from a conductor or graphic score, to create an expressive piece; eg adjusts playing to follow crescendo and diminuendo music symbols on a score.

Lower Key stage 1 (including nursery/reception/pupils with PMLD)

- Contrasting loud-soft music in juxtaposition, where there is a marked distinction. (NB seek advice on suitability of this with certain pupils who may be shocked into spasm.)
- Listening and responding to loud and soft music – do the pupils indicate a preference?
- Using the volume control on a keyboard, cassette recorder, radio, loud-hailer, etc.
- Using the microphone to enlarge pupils' vocalisations.

Upper Key stage 1

Continue developing the above, in addition:

- Establishing contrasting concepts of loud/quiet sounds – use arms outstretched for loud and close to for quiet – playing or singing quietly or loudly.
- Singing known familiar songs loudly or quietly, maybe varying within the song: eg quiet verse, loud chorus.
- Work on instruments: producing different sounds on same instrument: eg tapping tambour lightly with fingers to produce quiet sound, then using beater to produce louder sounds.
- Using instruments that are inherently loud or quiet: eg cowbell (loud) and triangle (quiet).
- Muffling familiar loud sounds under cushions or in cupboard (eg noisy clock); play 'hunt the noisemaker' where a pupil has to seek out the sound source.
- Play 'hot and cold' to find a noisemaker: when the seeker is 'hot', group to clap loudly – when 'cold', clap quietly.

Lower Key stage 2

Continue developing the above, in addition:

- Gradations of volume: control of voice and playing, getting louder and getting quieter on visual cue (eg arms opening and closing). NB louder to softer will be more challenging.
- Grouping instruments according to whether inherently loud or quiet.
- Doing familiar activities as quietly as possible. Also, activities that are difficult to carry out quietly: eg opening a packet of crisps, eating celery, passing a balloon round without making any sound at all. This is to teach that it takes *effort* to produce a quiet sound. Follow up with a musical activity: eg can a pupil then play a cymbal using a beater *quietly?*
- Using percussion instruments that can be played both loudly and quietly, to challenge the pupils to produce the required effect.

Upper Key stage 2/3

Continue developing the above, in addition:

- Adapting playing to balance the sounds being produced within the group: eg so that the tune is not drowned by the drummers' accompaniment.
- Using instruments that demand more complex motoric skill to control dynamics, including pitched instruments (eg chime bars), played with one or two beaters.
- Awareness of sounds that are close to (loud) and those that are distant (quiet), and those that graduate (eg a car approaching). Incorporate these ideas into a group composition.
- Notating scores (graphic and traditional) to indicate changes in dynamics and emphasis.

- Practising and performing a percussion part, changing level of loudness as required on visual cue from conductor and/or from notation on score.
- Controlling the voice to sing confidently and with lyrical expression.

Tempo

Tempo gives pace and speed to a piece of music. It is affected by physical co-ordination and the complexity of an instrument. For example, playing a drum fast and smoothly using alternate beaters is more difficult than playing fast on maracas. Pupils with learning difficulties may perseverate at a particular tempo; they need to be challenged gradually to develop an awareness of different speeds. Selective use of tempo can generate feelings of excitement and calm; pupils need to develop an awareness of this expressive potential.

> *Long-term aim:*
> To control singing and playing with the necessary physical co-ordination to maintain a steady pulse at different speeds, towards achieving an expressive quality to music-making.
>
> *Short-term objectives:*
> 1. Shows awareness of extremes in tempo; eg responds to abrupt change in speed at which a familiar song is performed (eg Heads, Shoulders, Knees and Toes).
> 2. Adjusts playing to accompaniment with marked changes in pace, not necessarily keeping in time; eg plays fast along to extract from Rossini's 'William Tell', then slow to extract from Dvorak's 'New World Symphony'.
> 3. Adjusts playing to accompaniment with a subtle change in pace, keeping in time; eg follows teacher's changes in pace to illustrate events in the song 'The Train is a-coming', slowing down and quickening at appropriate moments.
> 4. Gradually quickens the pace to create an accelerando; eg adjusts playing or singing gradually to get faster on cue from the conductor.
> 5. Gradually slows down to create a rallentando; eg adjusts playing or singing to slow down gradually on cue from the conductor.
> 6. Copes with sudden and/or gradual changes in speed on cue, to create an expressive piece; eg from a conductor or on a visual score, or following variations in pulse as controlled by the kendang (drum) in gamelan playing (Javanese percussion orchestra).

Lower Key stage 1 (including nursery/reception/pupils with PMLD)

- Listening and responding in movement to changes in tempo (speed), through the medium of adult supporting as necessary (aim to fade out).
- Contrasting actions to a song/piece of music with fast-slow sections.
- Using instruments/body sounds (eg clapping, stamping) to respond to changes in tempo.
- Visual reinforcement of varied playing: eg puppet or member of staff dancing smoothly to slow accompaniment (live or taped music) contrasted with jerky dancing for fast sections.

Upper Key stage 1

Continue developing the above, in addition:

- Establishing contrasting concepts of fast/slow – teacher to use obvious arm movements and gestures to indicate which is required.
- Pupils to respond to fast/slow music and changes of tempo, through movement and contrasting actions.
- Choosing appropriate songs to illustrate speeds – link with animal that moves slowly or quickly, traffic accelerating, etc.
- Singing and/or accompanying a song slowly or quickly, maybe varying the tempo within a song (eg slow verse, contrasted with fast chorus).

Lower Key stage 2

Continue developing the above, in addition:

- Exploring gradations of speed using simple percussion that will not impede control, to reflect an idea in music: eg leaves blowing, a car accelerating, aeroplane taking off.
- Introduce notion of reducing speed (this is harder to control): eg traffic approaching lights, train coming to station, a top finishing its spin; use visual stimulus.
- Pupils to adapt playing according to gradations of speed within a piece of music (live or taped music).
- Adjusting playing on visual cue from conductor (teacher or pupil), to produce fast/slow sections.

Upper Key stage 2/3

Continue developing the above, in addition:

- Responding to changes in music – sudden or gradual – by adjusting playing or singing.
- Using keyboard buttons to control tempo (speed) – adjusted by pupil.
- Notating required speed on a score: eg inventing symbols to indicate fast/slow and gradations.
- Practising and performing a percussion part, adjusting speed as required on visual cue from conductor and/or from notation on score.

Pitch

Without pitch, music is all on one level. High and low sounds give music its melody and harmony. This cannot be achieved on all instruments – many percussion instruments are unpitched, although adjusting the tension of skins on drums may give a slightly different tone. Certain basic percussion instruments (eg agogo bells, and toned wood blocks) will provide different pitches, although some pupils may find these difficult to discriminate. Pitched instruments usually refer to those on which it is possible to play a scale (or part of a scale) – eg xylophone, metallophone, chime bars, glockenspiel, keyboard, piano, recorders, guitar, chromaharp. The black notes of a keyboard form the notes of the five-note 'pentatonic' scale, which features in folk music across many cultures. For classroom work, the following versions of the scale are commonly used in pitched accompaniments and compositions with pitch:

```
C D E   G A
F G A   C D
G A B   D E
```

Pupils may harness their growing awareness of how pitches may be combined in playing, and extend their vocal range, to contribute to their ability to express themselves through music. Pupils may invent their own shortened scales (eg C E F G), to create different effects.

Long-term aim:
To recognise the significance of changing levels in high/low sounds, to give expression and a lyrical quality to a piece of music.

Short-term objectives:
1. Shows awareness of extremes in high/low singing or playing; eg responds to his/her name being sung by the teacher at unfamiliar pitches.
2. Relates to distinct concepts of high/low in teacher-led music activities; eg moves hands up and down appropriately in 'Hickory Dickory Dock'; selects an appropriate instrument or sings high/low to illustrate an episode in a story, such as growling or playing a bass drum for a big dog, and a high yap or playing a small triangle for a small dog.
3. Is aware of a possible range in high/low sounds that affect the quality of a piece of music; eg matches glissandos in singing and/or playing instruments to an accompaniment with noticeable rises and falls in melody.
4. Translates a required sound pattern (ostinato) involving two or more pitches into playing and/or singing; eg selects appropriate chime bars from a limited range to imitate and sustain the sound of a fire engine: G-E or F-D, etc.
5. Discriminates subtle distinctions in pitch to produce a familiar melody; eg performs a well-known song by singing tunefully or picking out the melody on a pitched instrument.
6. Combines pitched sounds instrumentally or vocally to produce an intended effect; eg composes a piece involving two or more pitched instruments that harmonise together and which could be 'fixed' on a score.

Lower Key stage 1 (nursery/reception/pupils with PMLD)

- Teacher and supporting staff vocalising high-low (eg pupils' names, open vowel sounds, glissando/sliding sounds up and down), using hands as visual reinforcement.
- Using tuned instruments: eg playing piano on high notes then low notes, swanee whistle; responding through movement with support as necessary, to changes in pitch.
- Using music technology to reinforce high/low singing (eg of pupils' names) or vocalisations; play sounds back to pupils. Reactions?
- Listening to live or taped music, with contrasting high/low sections in juxtaposition. Preferences?
- Developing an awareness of when a sound is 'wrong': eg teacher deliberately playing a wrong note in a familiar tune. Reactions?

Upper Key stage 1

Continue developing the above, in addition:

- Establishing concepts of high/low through songs that go up and down, eg 'Jack and Jill', 'Grand Old Duke of York' (although this does not actually go up and down in the right places).
- Inventing stories to illustrate obvious high/low, and glissando (gradations up and down) using sounds on instruments to match.
- Up-ending manageable xylophone/metallophone to indicate step by step playing (remove surplus or impeding bars) and glissando. Child to copy: eg 'Ted-dy's climb-ing up the lad-der' – or sliding down the banister!
- Encouraging awareness of high/low speaking voices: use puppets to indicate which kind of voice to use (eg Mr Whisper, Mrs Sing); imitating animal sounds (big dog compared to little dog, baby lamb compared to mother ewe, etc).
- Encourage singing their names on more than one note: eg 'Da-vid', moving from high to low, in musical repartee (eg hello song).
- Encourage singing of familiar songs: eg joining in a familiar refrain.
- Exploring a range of varied consonants and vowels (speech sounds), varying the pitch high or low.

Lower Key stage 2

Continue developing the above, in addition:

- Extending vocal range through long open vowels (voice work): gesture to indicate sound on one note, then gesture up and down to produce waves of high and low sounds.
- Teacher using gestures and hand movements as visual reinforcement of pitch in familiar songs, pupils to copy. NB teacher to lead using a pitch a few tones higher than normal speaking voice.
- Teacher singing questions: pupils to respond 'no' using low note or 'yes' using high note – singing or playing response (eg low drum, high cymbal crash).

- Controlled sequential playing of tuned percussion (eg single chime bars), skill of bouncing beater. Group turn-taking activities playing chords on chime bars: A-C-E C-E-G G-B-D D-F-A or any combination of black notes.
- Simple ostinato playing on pitched instrument: eg fire engine: G-E-G-E (adult to support or prompt as necessary – aim to fade out).
- Singing more sustained melodic phrases and with developing confidence, in familiar tunes.

Upper Key stage 2/3

Continue developing the above, in addition:

- Finding the same note when singing with others; matching to a drone at different pitches.
- Maintaining a more complex ostinato on a pitched instrument (three notes or more) – aim to fade out adult support.
- Imitating open-throat singing and pitched material: eg market cries, football chants; develop into new material and repartee.
- Introducing a stave (initially one line) on which to indicate high and low sounds (above/below the line). Develop up to the traditional five-line stave.
- Adjusting singing in response to visual cue from conductor and/or on score – loudly, quietly, slowly, quickly, as well as high and/or low.

INDIVIDUAL PROGRESS IN THE MUSIC ELEMENTS

Name..........................

Class..........................

1 → 6
begun   acquired

Date..........................
Comments, Observations, Future Priorities

- Ability to understand and use TIMBRE: the quality of sound
- Ability to understand and use TEXTURE: the density of sound
- Ability to understand and use DURATION: the length of sound
- Ability to understand and use SILENCE: the space between sounds
- Ability to understand and use DYNAMICS: sound levels (loud, quiet, etc)
- Ability to understand and use TEMPO: the pace and speed of sounds
- Ability to understand and use PITCH: sound levels (high, low, etc)

Date..........................
Comments, Observations, Future Priorities

Date..........................
Comments, Observations, Future Priorities

Date..........................
Comments, Observations, Future Priorities

- Ability to understand and use TIMBRE: the quality of sound
- Ability to understand and use TEXTURE: the density of sound
- Ability to understand and use DURATION: the length of sound
- Ability to understand and use SILENCE: the space between sounds
- Ability to understand and use DYNAMICS: sound levels (loud, quiet, etc)
- Ability to understand and use TEMPO: the pace and speed of sounds
- Ability to understand and use PITCH: sound levels (high, low, etc)

CHAPTER 5

Towards Composition – Structuring Music

This chapter will consider ways to enable pupils of all abilities to arrange their music-making to achieve a composition. Essentially, a composition may be regarded as a series of sounds that have been given shape with a beginning, middle and an end. Structure may be considered on different levels, for example: from starting and stopping on cue, to playing a simple ostinato (repeated pattern) of two sounds with its own intrinsic structure, to a composition with several sections. Structure in music is achieved through the use of: *repetition, pattern*, and *contrast*.

Music can be a transient art form, and therefore literally needs to be 'fixed' in some way. The most obvious means to do this in the classroom is for the teacher to have a cassette recorder with tape at the ready, so that a piece of work can instantly be recorded and played back to the pupils. Many pupils with learning difficulties benefit from this immediate experience, and may struggle with recall otherwise. They may need to hear the piece at least twice through before they begin to absorb significant elements. They need to learn to become 'active listeners'; giving them something specific to focus on is useful, eg 'would any part of the music sound better played more quietly?'. Feeding back even an unpromising series of sounds to the pupils may be a useful springboard for improving the quality: the pupils may be prompted into considering their work critically, in order to offer comments on ways to refine the sounds.

Teachers inevitably have ultimate responsibility at all ability levels for helping pupils to shape their work. With pupils with learning difficulties, the boundaries within which they are to make creative decisions may need to be quite narrowly defined. This may seem as if the teacher is being over-prescriptive in helping the pupils to structure their work. However, paradoxically, they may need this narrow focus in order actually to engage in divergent thinking – to make a creative decision. Parameters within which pupils are to make creative choices may be gradually broadened. Pupils' creative ideas may need considerable teasing out by the teacher, and may need sensitive timing and skilled questioning on the part of the teacher. 'Closed' questions, even those requiring a yes/no response, may potentially lead to a creative idea. For example: a non-verbal pupil may be asked to decide if he or she would like

TOWARDS COMPOSITION
Development in Structuring Music

There may be four aspects involved in structuring music at all stages of development

1 – *controlling sounds*
2 – *performing with others*
3 – *composing*
4 – *refining, recording and communicating musical ideas*

Lower Key Stage 1: **Reactive**
creating patterns of sound as part of the group
1 exploring a possible range of sounds with staff support – blowing, plucking, shaking, tapping, scraping activities on instruments and in the environment
2 participating in group music-making with staff support
3 structured improvisation between clearly demarcated silences
4 indicating preferred sounds – recording work on tape

Upper Key Stage 1: **Active**
shaping patterns of sound as part of the group
1 basic contrasts on classroom percussion requiring non-complex motoric skill – making a single sound from an instrument or sound-maker, by shaking, tapping, blowing or scraping
2 turn-taking as part of the group on cue from conductor (teacher or pupil)
3 compositions with a two-part structure (A-B), with strongly contrasting sounds that repeat
4 recording work on tape (listen and rework); use of picture symbols/visual cues to reinforce the musical pattern

Lower Key Stage 2: **Interactive**
refining patterns of sound within smaller groupings
1 gradations of contrast on instruments demanding more complex motoric skill – making more than one sound from an instrument or sound-maker
2 turn-taking in groups – maintaining their part alongside peers
3 composing pieces with two/three part structure (A-B-A) with more subtle contrasts
4 recording work on tape (listen and rework); use of graphic symbols to score work (eg writing patterns) to indicate when to play

Upper Key Stage 2/3: **Proactive**
developing patterns of sound for others to play
1 using a range of contrasting sounds on familiar and unfamiliar sound sources
2 using a range of permutations on solo/ensemble playing for effect
3 composing pieces with more complex patterning (eg rondo: A-B-A-C-A)
4 recording work on tape (listen and rework); precise graphic scoring to indicate wehen and how to play; possible use of traditional notation to indicate length of sounds and relative pitch

Figure 5.1

there to be drums in the group piece – indicating yes/no by signing or gesture will significantly affect the outcome.

The figure summarises development in structuring music across the Key stages. As with the summary figure in Chapter 4, four stages of development have been identified, together with broad descriptive characteristics.

Performing With Others

Long-term aim:
To participate in group music-making, vocally and/or instrumentally, realising the significance of his/her contribution.

Short-term objectives:
1. Makes a sound on encouragement from the teacher; eg vocalises when the teacher makes a distinct speech sound, such as 'sshhhh'.
2. Is aware when music starts and stops in group music activity; eg joins in playing or singing to the sound of the accompaniment.
3. Responds to a cue from a conductor to start and stop in ensemble playing or singing; eg watches for conductor's hands open/closed to indicate start/stop, and co-ordinates playing of instrument accordingly.
4. Maintains his/her part by taking turns in group music making activities; eg appreciates his/her contribution in a group piece by playing or singing only on the conductor's cue.
5. Plays or sings as part of a section to produce a unison sound; eg adjusts playing or singing to match that of peers maintaining the same part in a familiar tune.
6. Is able to sustain his/her part whether in solo/ensemble playing or singing, to achieve a particular effect; eg maintains a vocal part in a round.

Controlling Sounds

Long-term aim:
To play a variety of instruments with the necessary skills and/or use the voice over an extended range, in order to achieve a variety of possible musical sounds.

Short-term objectives:
1. Discovers sounds can be reproduced; eg repeatedly bangs table top, large drum, etc.
2. Realises sounds can be produced in different ways by playing basic instruments appropriately; eg shakes maraca, taps drum, scrapes guiro, blows duck call, etc.
3. Produces distinctly contrasting sounds using voice and/or basic percussion; eg sings and/or plays loudly/quietly, fast/slow, high/low.
4. Produces gradations of contrasting sounds using voice and/or basic percussion; eg sings and/or plays getting faster/slower, louder/quieter, higher/lower.
5. Plays with subtlety on instruments demanding more complex motoric skill; eg plays metallophone with two beaters, alternates left/right hand playing on drum, picks out required notes on a glockenspiel, etc.
6. Selects instrument and style of playing and/or singing to express an idea in music; eg chooses a slow steady crescendo drum beat for the giant's footsteps, with a quick descending scale on a glockenspiel for Jack climbing down the beanstalk.

Composing

Long-term aim:
To combine musical sounds within a structured framework to devise an original piece with a clear beginning, middle and end.

Short-term objectives:
1. Indicates a preference for particular sounds to be contained within clearly demarcated silences controlled by the teacher in a group improvised piece; eg reacts positively to a trill on the triangle, but expresses dislike at the sound of a cowbell.
2. Selects preferred instrument from a limited choice to play on cue from a teacher's signal to start and stop in a class improvised piece; eg chooses a maraca in preference to a drum.
3. Pupil gives shape to a structured improvisation by deciding when musicians are to play or sing in a group improvised piece; eg conducts players by randomly indicating stop – play – stop.
4. Decides when and how to introduce basic contrasts to give shape and pattern to a group piece; eg devises a two-part structure (A–B), with alternating fast-slow playing of varying lengths of time, to represent a train arriving and departing from a station.
5. Includes more subtle contrasts to give shape and pattern to a group piece; eg devises a two or three part structure, with slow legato playing followed by fast staccato playing, maybe with a slow legato section to finish.
6. Suggests more complex patterning (eg rondo A-B-A-C-A) to create a more involved piece; eg chooses basic percussion instruments to represent general traffic noise (quiet ensemble playing – A), B to represent solo traffic hooter on a duck call, and C to represent a sudden intrusion of a solo ostinato fire engine on recorder notes E-G.

Refining, Recording and Communicating Musical Ideas

Long-term aim:
To share music-making with others with an awareness of audience, venue and occasion, through presenting work live or previously recorded on tape.

Short-term objectives:
1. Reacts to the sound of own music-making being replayed immediately; eg smiles at his/her spontaneous vocalisation reinforced by echo-microphone.
2. Conveys a basic musical idea in a teacher-led activity; eg plays a simple percussion instrument on cue fast, slow, loudly, quietly.
3. Listens to music-making being replayed on tape, and suggests ways of changing the sounds to create an effect; eg suggests playing a piece quietly with a loud beat at the end.
4. Uses visual cues to sequence musical ideas to be recorded on tape, then listened to and modified; eg picture of a person felling a tree followed by a picture of a tree crashing down, as prompts for solo drum and group of tambourines, for a piece that could subsequently have fast-slow, loud-soft concepts introduced.
5. Uses graphic symbols to score a composition to be recorded on tape and subsequently modified, to indicate when different instruments are to play; eg sequences writing pattern cards (OOOOO llllllllll OOOOO), where OOOO represents wooden instruments , and llllllllll represents glissandos and trills on metal instruments.
6. Uses more precise graphic scoring and/or basic traditional notation to devise a composition to be recorded on tape and subsequently modified and rehearsed, with a view to possible live performance to an audience; eg indicates when and how different instruments are to play in a group piece about the countryside:

on-going shakers (trees swaying)	eeeeeeeeee
intermittent drum (dog barking)	llll llll llll
intermittent solo wood block (small dog)	iiii iiii iiii
intermittent cuckoo call	notated around a single line E
	G

Lower Key stage 1 (including nursery/reception and pupils with PMLD)

- *Controlling sounds:* Exploring a possible range of sounds with staff support on basic classroom percussion with large playing surfaces, and sounds in the immediate environment (eg on table top, floor, knees, radiator, etc).
- *Performing with others:* Participating in group music-making experiences with staff supporting as necessary.
- *Composing:* Exploring possibilities with sound in structured improvisation between clearly demarcated silences.
- *Refining, recording and communicating musical ideas:* Record work on tape – enhance through sound processors and effects units, etc.

This stage in music-making is equivalent to the scribbling stage in art development. The pupils' spontaneous music therefore will be a medley of exploratory improvisation. Teachers need to find ways to give this structure and shape. The simplest way is to give this form through a clear start and stop signal. Supporting staff will have a critical role therefore in 'defining' the sounds between these two moments of silence. Pupils should be encouraged to work towards responding to a cue to start and stop. The obvious way is through the conductor's (teacher or pupil) gestures: hands together – hands open and sign Makaton for 'play' – hands close to stop. Alternatively, pupils may learn to respond to other forms of cue: eg using lights on/off, projecting images onto a wall that start and stop, etc.

Variety and quality may be introduced through drawing on the key components of repetition, pattern and contrast. Essentially these will be two-part patterns that repeat, with different styles of contrast.

For example:

- Play – stop – play – stop … repeated blocks of sound-making.
- Solo instrument – everybody play – solo instrument – everybody play.
- Shaking sounds that get louder – shaking sounds that get quieter.
- Fast playing – slow playing – fast playing – slow playing.
- High glissandos on glockenspiel or wind chimes – low playing on keyboard/piano or bass metallophone/xylophone.
- Shaking sounds – tapping sounds.
- Open vowel sound – pupil's name – open vowel sound – pupil's name.

Upper Key stage 1

- *Controlling sounds:* Basic contrasts – fast/slow, high/low, loud/quiet, solo/ensemble – on basic classroom percussion requiring non-complex motoric skill (eg tambourine, jingle bells, drum, etc).
- *Performing with others:* Turn-taking as part of the group on cue from conductor (teacher or pupil).
- *Composing:* Two-part structure (A – B) with strongly contrasting sounds that repeat to produce a pattern.
- *Refining, recording and communicating musical ideas:* Record work on tape, listen and rework – refining sounds through introducing marked contrast – use of picture symbols or coloured bricks as visual cues to reinforce pattern.

At this stage, pupils need to develop greater awareness of pattern within the context of the group, with respect for turn-taking. A group composition may be exploration of the music elements, or expressing a simple idea in sound. Pupils will have emerging control over basic percussion instruments demanding non-complex motoric skill (eg tambourines, maracas, jingle bells, etc). This should be developed and harnessed within group composition. Pupils' creative ideas and decisions may relate to selecting a preferred way of playing, or preferred instruments or numbers of instruments.

For example:

- Establish on-going pattern using body sounds: eg slap knees, clap hands.
- Relate ideas of a repeating pattern by using coloured bricks, patterns on clothing, etc.
- Divide group into two, with staff supporting in each: group A clap, group B slap knees.
- Pupil to pick up instrument in controlled fashion and keep still until his/her turn to play – each child to have a turn to play under the teacher's direction.
- Develop simple two-part pattern (musical 'conversation') using simple instruments or vocal work.
- Explore within the two-part structure: eg conductor (teacher or pupil) with cue cards holds up picture of drums – all the drums play; then STOP when card is put down; pupil holds up picture of bells, etc.
- Pupil holds up picture of dog – drums play; then holds up picture of cat – triangles play ... etc.
- Two sounds on different instruments: how can we change it? Record, play back.

Lower Key stage 2

- *Controlling sounds:* Gradations of contrast – more subtlety – on instruments demanding more complex motoric skill (eg cabasa, cow bell, co-ordinating two beaters, two-tone wood block, etc).
- *Performing with others:* Turn-taking in groups: pupils maintain their part alongside peers.
- *Composing:* Two to three part structure (A-B-A) with more subtle contrasts.
- *Refining, recording and communicating musical ideas:* Record on tape, listen and rework: graphic symbols (eg writing patterns oooo llllll oooo) to score a composition to indicate when to play.

At this stage, pupils will be developing greater versatility in their playing, with more control over their instruments, finer touch and growing sensitivity. They will be more capable therefore of managing percussion instruments that present challenges with regard to the degree of control required. In structuring their music-making, the teacher could usefully set a clear basic pulse to keep the improvisation together. Composition may be developed from a two-part structure to a piece with three clear sections. Each section could reflect more in-depth exploration of the music elements: either abstract work or maybe to express an idea or to illustrate a story through the music. Pupils may benefit paradoxically from having *fewer* instruments, in order to encourage more varied playing and prevent distraction: they may be more able then to concentrate on developing musical patterns and a range of sounds from one instrument.

For example:

- Pupils to sustain a simple ostinato (repeated pattern) of two sounds for a length of time.
- 'Musical sandwiches' using instruments and vocal sounds: A – B – A (pupils suggest different 'fillings' for B: eg wooden instruments – metal instruments – wooden instruments.
- Three sounds played in a sequence: how can we change it? (dynamics? order of playing? speed? etc).
- Making up a story: eg choose two animals – make up a simple episode.
- One instrument – play three different sounds – develop into a story.
- Two actions that one creature does – develop into repeated pattern: A-B-A-B.
- Illustrating a story or picture – link sounds to represent images in a sequence.

Upper Key stage 2/3

- *Controlling sounds:* Use of a range of contrasts to express ideas in music.
- *Performing with others:* Range of permutations on solo/ensemble playing to achieve a particular effect.
- *Composing:* More complex patterning (eg rondo: A – B – A – C – A) to link to an idea/story to be expressed through the music.
- *Refining, recording and communicating musical ideas:* Record on tape, listen and rework; more precise graphic scoring to indicate when and how to play: eg oooOOOOO lll lll lll lll OOOOOOoooo; possible introduction of basic notation to indicate length of a sound (quaver, crotchet, minim) and relative pitch.

At this stage, pupils need to transfer their growing ability to control their playing onto instruments that are more fragile, unusual and sophisticated. In addition to setting a pulse, the teacher could encourage pupils to work to a simple rhythm: eg <u>dum</u>-di-di – <u>dum</u>-di-di – <u>dum</u> – di -di… Pupils may be able to cope with more sections within the structure of the composition – maybe A-B-C-B-A or a rondo form: A-B-A-C-A, for example, where A is everyone playing together, and B and C represent solo parts. More attention needs to be given not only to *when* they are to play, but also *how* they are to play, to achieve greater expression within the context of the group. For example, sudden sounds, fading sounds, pauses, rests will also need to be indicated when scoring a piece of work. Consideration needs to be given to the required mood (eg a sad piece) or narrative, and how this can be achieved through ordering different combinations of solo or ensemble playing in sequence. Some pupils with learning difficulties may find it problematic to generate creative ideas in small groups without adult support. Nevertheless, at this stage, as far as possible, opportunity should be given for pupils to have ownership of an original piece of work that has been composed in a small group (with an adult sensitively supporting as necessary) as well as in whole group music-making.

For example:

- Adding on to the end of a story, to complete it in music.
- Everyday routines described in music, eg brushing teeth.
- Original story board in pictures, retold in music.
- Familiar song, story, poem or event expressed in music.
- Four sounds played in a sequence: how can we change it to make it more interesting?
- More complex ostinato playing over three notes or more (on chime bars, keyboard, etc), co-ordinating one or two-handed playing.
- Composing and scoring a piece to be played by others, using graphic scoring (eg pictures or writing patterns) or basic notation.
- Composing a piece of music for a specific purpose (eg as accompaniment for dance) taking account of length of time required for particular sections.
- Capturing a spontaneous composition (eg pupil randomly 'conducts' musicians when to play) by recording on tape, listening and refining the work, and then scoring it, maybe for others to play.

INDIVIDUAL PROGRESS IN COMPOSING MUSIC

Name..................

Class..................

1 → 6
begun   acquired

Date..................
Comments, Observations, Future Priorities

Ability to perform with others: to participate in group music-making

Ability to control sounds: to achieve a variety of possible musical sounds

Ability to compose: to combine musical sounds within a structured framework

Ability to refine, record and communicate musical ideas: to share music-making

Date..................
Comments, Observations, Future Priorities

Date..................
Comments, Observations, Future Priorities

Ability to perform with others: to participate in group music-making

Ability to control sounds: to achieve a variety of possible musical sounds

Ability to compose: to combine musical sounds within a structured framework

Ability to refine, record and communicate musical ideas: to share music-making

Date..................
Comments, Observations, Future Priorities

CHAPTER 6

Learning to Listen – Listening to and Appraising Music

This chapter will consider strategies for enabling pupils of all abilities to appreciate and respond to music and sound through *active listening*. This may embrace not only music of established composers, but also the pupils' own compositions. Making and appraising music should be inter-related, with opportunities seized to reinforce both aspects. Sounds should be played *and* heard: the teacher needs to find ways to 'capture' the sound to be re-played to the pupils, either 'live' or on tape. Having a cassette recorder to hand, with a blank tape ready, is useful in music-making with pupils at all ability levels, so that any series of invented sounds can be instantly recorded, listened to, then reworked and refined.

Pupils' awareness of different kinds of music needs to be developed and expanded through listening to performances, both 'live' and pre-recorded on tape. Pupils need to be exposed to a wide range of musical styles, culturally and historically. Concepts of time and place may be problematic for many pupils with learning difficulties. Often however, it can suffice to tell the pupils that a particular piece of music comes from (eg) 'a long way away across the sea', or 'was made up a long time ago, before Granny was born' or 'in the days when people wore clothes like in this picture' or 'when there were no televisions, cars or microwaves'. Teachers need to be critically aware of their own musical preferences, and avoid imposing their own musical taste or prejudices on the pupils.

The point of introducing pupils to different musical styles, therefore, is not to adopt a 'history of music' approach. Rather, it is to reinforce and complement the pupils' own music-making, and to offer inspiration and enjoyment from their musical heritage. For example, listening to extracts of music may link with a musical pattern that pupils are exploring on instruments: they may listen for crescendos in any Rossini overture, and then make a gradual 'roar' using voice or instruments, getting louder and then quieter.

Opportunities should be made to explore resources available in the community. Pupils may be taken to concerts, making use of disabled facilities (eg wheelchair access and sound loops); many venues are now adopting a consciously positive attitude to people with special needs. Many professional musicians welcome the opportunity to perform to pupils in schools – this may

DEVELOPMENT IN LEARNING TO LISTEN

The following aspects may be addressed in developing active listening at each stage:
1 – *how sounds are made*
2 – *how sounds are used for expressive effect*
3 – *the cultural and historical base*
4 – *responding to the mood*
5 – *communicating feelings and ideas*

Lower Key Stage 1: **Reactive**
reacting to a range of familiar musical sounds
1 exploring sounds through blowing, shaking, tapping, scraping activities
2 associating sounds and music with visual and tactile reinforcers, eg pictorial cues
3 associating a piece of music with its origin through multi-sensory reinforcers
4 responding to an extract through an associated activity – art, dance, drink, time etc
5 spontaneous positive and/or negative responses to different kinds of music

Upper Key Stage 1: **Active**
recognising a range of familiar musical sounds
1 awareness of how to make a single sound by tapping, scraping, blowing or shaking
2 identifying sounds in a sequence towards recognising musical patterns
3 active recall of a musical experience
4 controlled responses to different kinds of music with definite contrasts
5 consciously relating to familiar sounds

Lower Key Stage 2: **Interactive**
reacting to a range of familiar and unfamiliar musical sounds
1 awareness of more than one possible sound from an instrument or sound-maker
2 understanding how sounds can be combined to achieve a particular effect
3 interactive response to hearing music from other times and cultures
4 developing structured responses to basic moods conveyed in music
5 consciously relating to familiar and unfamiliar musical/sound experiences

Upper Key Stage 2/3: **Proactive**
recognising a range of familiar and unfamiliar musical sounds
1 discriminating sounds produced in a similar way from familiar and unfamiliar sources
2 wider appreciation of the use of sounds in combination, including abstract ideas
3 association of a piece of music with a particular time and culture
4 understanding the way a composer has created a mood in music
5 considering how music can be used to express an idea or feelings

Figure 6.1

offer additional follow-up possibilities to handle the instruments and talk with the artists. Links with local high schools and contacts with arts support services may provide ready access to wider resources (eg orchestras, steel bands, gamelan, etc). A local music librarian will usually be able to suggest appropriate taped music for a particular requirement; for instance, 'have you got anything on the theme of the seasons?' may yield Vivaldi's 'The Seasons', Stravinsky's 'Rite of Spring', Gershwin's 'Summertime', Mungo Jerry's 'In the Summertime', and 'Sunny Afternoon' by the Kinks. Additionally, several educational compilation tapes and packs of different kinds of musical extracts are now available (see appendix of Resources).

The figure summarises development in learning to listen across the key stages. As with the summary figures in Chapters 4 and 5, four stages of development have been identified, together with broad characteristic descriptors.

How Sounds Are Made

Long-term aim:
To distinguish and recognise different types of sounds in a piece of music, appreciating how they have been produced.

Short-term objectives:
1. Is able to produce involuntary sounds on a range of noisemakers, by shaking or banging; eg gamelan gong.
2. Consciously explores sound properties of a range of objects/ instruments; eg rainmaker tube, chicken bones, dried orange peel castanets, etc.
3. Is able to produce an appropriate sound on a basic percussion instrument; eg shakes maraca, taps tambour, scrapes guiro, blows nightingale call.
4. Is able to produce more than one sound from a basic percussion instrument; eg shakes, taps, scrapes tambourine.
5. Is able to produce sounds appropriately from unfamiliar instruments/ noisemakers; eg double agogo, shekere.
6. Recognises how sounds are produced in pre-recorded music; eg discriminates a solo brass instrument from string accompaniment/ ensemble background playing.

Lower Key stage 1 (including nursery/reception and pupils with PMLD)
Exploring sounds through blowing, plucking and shaking activities – sounds made by pupils and/or supporting staff.

For example:

- Use of attractive sound-makers (different textures, colours, etc).
- Making sounds in the environment (scraping stick along a radiator, etc).
- Listening to body sounds (clapping, stamping, rubbing, etc).
- Blowing through a tube (into water or across the top of a whirly tube).
- Running fingers across a guitar or chromaharp.

Upper Key stage 1

Continue developing the above, in addition:

Conscious awareness of how to make a single sound from an instrument or sound-maker.

For example:

- Use of songs to teach a basic music vocabulary: shake, tap, blow, scrape.
- Identifying an instrument played behind a screen by finding matching partner from a selection on the table.
- Identifying a common solo instrument within the pupil's range of experience (eg piano, drum, guitar).
- Listening and identifying sounds in the environment, eg toilet flushing, footsteps, doorbell, telephone, the sea, wind, etc.

Lower Key stage 2

Continue developing the above, in addition:

Ability to make more than one sound from an instrument or sound-maker.

For example:

- Use of songs demanding a variety of sounds from an instrument: eg shaking tambourine to 'one-a-penny two-a-penny', then tapping tambourine to 'hot cross buns'.
- Identifying a more complex percussion instrument played behind a screen, with matching partner from selection on table (eg cabasa, tongue or slit drum, agogo bells).
- Listening to and identifying two instruments playing a duet (behind a screen or on tape): eg xylophone with a drum, piano and violin, tambourine and chime bars.
- Recognising like sounds in ensemble playing (themselves on tape, as well as groups in performance): eg wooden instruments, metal instruments, bagpipes, brass band.

Upper Key stage 2/3

Continue developing the above, in addition:

Discriminating sounds that are produced in a similar way from familiar and unfamiliar sources.

For example:

- Identifying 'plugged' and 'unplugged' (electronic/acoustic) music.
- Using keyboard buttons to alter the tone of a sound: eg trumpets, violin, flute.

- Listening to groups or 'families' of instruments: eg in the orchestra (strings, woodwind, brass), steel bands, brass bands, recorder ensembles.
- Indicating how an unusual instrument might be played: eg whether plucked, blown, strummed, tapped, etc.

How Sounds Are Used For Effect

> *Long-term aim:*
> To understand a composer's ideas expressed in a piece of music, by appreciating the way sounds have been used.
>
> *Short-term objectives:*
> 1. Responds to extremes of dynamics and tempo; eg becomes excited when listening to a rousing piece.
> 2. Consciously engages with a multi-sensory experience, linking stimuli with intended imagery in a piece of music; eg tape-slide show of Turner's sea paintings to accompaniment of appropriate music on sea theme, reflecting corresponding calm and storm.
> 3. Realises different outcomes from playing instruments in different ways; eg banging a drum loudly to shock or surprise, exerting fine touch on wind chimes to achieve a soothing effect.
> 4. Understands that music can be used to illustrate an idea; eg participates in group story-making, using classroom instruments to relate the narrative.
> 5. Realises the effect that a piece of prerecorded music has, by describing a suitable context where it could be performed; eg disco dancing, church music, a lullaby, a march, etc.
> 6. Offers an interpretation for ideas encapsulated in a piece of music; eg invents a story for a piece of music with contrasting sections, such as the opening of Vaughan Williams' 'Sinfonia Antarctica.

Lower Key stage 1 (including nursery/reception/pupils with PMLD)

Linking sounds and music with reinforcers.

For example:

- Instruments/sound-makers with picture prompts: eg maraca with picture of the sea, slow drum beat with picture of elephant, warbler with picture of bird, etc.
- Using projected slides to accompany/illustrate a piece of music: eg Debussy's 'La Mer' with Turner paintings of the sea.
- Watching cartoons or animations, with expressive musical accompaniment: eg extracts from Disney's 'Fantasia' with Dukas' 'Sorcerer's Apprentice'.
- Tactile or textural prompts: eg running hands in water to accompaniment of 'Aquarium' in Saint-Saëns' 'Carnival of the Animals' (still water) or Smetana's 'Ma Vlast' (running water), feeling ice to Vaughan Williams' 'Antarctica', holding/exploring a pan-pipe to theme music of 'Flight of the Condor'.
- Exposing pupils to contrasting pieces of music in juxtaposition: eg music to soothe immediately contrasted with music to excite or rouse.
- Lighting to contrast: eg the calm before and after the storm in Beethoven's 'Pastoral Symphony', letting off fireworks to Tchaikowsky's '1812 Overture'.

Upper Key stage 1

Continue developing the above, in addition:

Identifying sounds in a sequence, towards recognising a pattern.

For example:

- Playing two instruments, one after the other: record, listen and re-play.
- Two-part story played on two kinds of instruments or voice work, with pictures as prompts: eg cat prowls around (drum beat) – cat chases mouse (claves) – record, listen and re-play.
- Listening to extracts of music with clear narrative: eg from Tchaikowsky's 'The Nutcracker'.
- Teacher to use appropriate music to settle or arouse pupils, as required!

Lower Key stage 2

Continue developing the above, in addition:

Understanding how sounds can be combined to achieve a particular effect.

For example:

- Selecting instruments from a limited choice to represent sounds in a story or in a picture: eg maracas to represent leaves rustling – listen, record, re-play.
- Recognising a motif in a piece of music: eg different characters in Prokofiev's 'Peter and the Wolf'.
- Listening to extracts of music with contrasting solo with ensemble playing – pupils to recognise whether one person/lots of people playing.
- Listening to extracts of contrasting types of music (eg band marching, lullaby, rock and roll) – pupils to match to an appropriate picture (soldiers on parade, baby, couple jiving).

Upper Key stage 2/3

Continue developing the above, in addition:

Use of sounds in combination for effect, including more abstract imagery.

For example:

- Listening to how different composers have created ethereal connotations: eg Holst's 'The Planets', '2001 Space Odyssey', 'Doctor Who', etc.
- Listening to theme music/incidental music used to accompany strong visual imagery in films/TV: eg cartoons, 'Chariots of Fire'.
- Composing class music to accompany an extract from a video.
- Comparing the impact of different combinations of instruments/voices across cultures: eg a solo bagpipe lament with African tribal chanting.

The Cultural and Historical Base

Long-term aim:
To recognise the significance of the origin and context of a piece of music, understanding that music comes from different times and places.

Short-term objectives:
1. Engages with music in a direct experience of a live performance; eg a visiting steel band, brass ensemble, etc.
2. Anticipates a familiar style from an associated stimulus; eg smiles at photo/ribbons/bells of Morris Dancers before being played taped music.
3. Recalls a musical experience; eg draws adult's attention to a picture in a book of an instrument which featured in a previous live performance.
4. Associates specific instruments with particular musical style; eg selects bongos to emulate African drumming, castanets for Spanish Flamenco, recorders for Elizabethan minstrels, etc.
5. Identifies a distinct piece of music according to its cultural source; eg recognises a raga from India, didgeridoo playing from Australia, bagpipes from Scotland, panpipes from South America, etc.
6. Locates a piece of music from another time with some awareness of how long ago it originated, according to a notional time-line; egs:
   - 70s Punk – 60s rock and roll – Wartime Swing – Dixieland traditional jazz – Strauss waltzes;
   - Weill's 'Threepenny Opera' – Wagner's 'Ring' – Beethoven's 'Pastoral Symphony' – Bach's 'Fugues'.

Lower Key stage 1 (including nursery/reception/pupils with PMLD)

Use of reinforcers to enable pupils to associate a piece of music with its origin.

For example:

- Musicians performing live (different kinds of instruments and styles): eg a string quartet, steel band.
- Use of costume: eg Morris dancers, Peruvian pan-pipe band, Early Music ensemble, clog dancers, etc.
- Pre-recorded performances on TV or video.
- Pictures and/or posters to link with a particular piece of music/genre.

Upper Key stage 1

Continue developing the above, in addition:

Active recall of a musical experience.

For example:

- Recognising an instrument used in a performance: eg from picture in book.
- Recalling a musical event through class photos.
- Recognising a piece of music heard on a previous significant occasion: eg digeridoo played in live performance, followed up with listening to Aboriginal music on tape in class.
- Replaying a musical experience on classroom instruments: eg tucking scraps of material into clothing and using claves and bells as Morris dancers.

Lower Key stage 2

Continue developing the above, in addition:

Interactive response to hearing music from other times and cultures.

For example:

- Harnessing the 'drone' feature in folk music across different cultures in class music-making: eg imitating bagpipe sound on kazoos or using voice.
- Matching pictures of musicians from different cultures/historical times with corresponding pieces of music.
- Beginning to associate extracts of music with its historical/cultural origin, where contrasts are very marked (pictures to prompt as necessary): eg Indian raga with African drumming or marimba-type instruments from Uganda.
- Identifying familiar instruments within the school in addition to basic classroom percussion: eg recorder, piano, guitar, violin.

Upper Key stage 2/3

Continue developing the above, in addition:

Conscious association of music with a particular time and culture.

For example:

- Identifying some unfamiliar instruments beyond the usual school experience: eg sitar, tabla drum, panpipes, Javanese gong, harp.
- Associating the materials from which an instrument is made with its likely origin: eg ethnic instruments crafted by hand compared with electronic keyboard.
- Associating types of music with moments in history: eg Wartime 'swing' (eg Glenn Miller), Medieval minstrels (eg recorders), '60s 'rock and roll'.
- Incorporating rhythmic elements from different cultures and times in class music making: eg using the cymbal to punctuate in gamelan music, playing in three-time as in a Viennese waltz.

Responding to the Mood of Music

Long-term aim:
To react to the evocative quality of a piece of music, reflecting a composer's ideas and intentions.

Short-term objectives:
1. Anticipates an activity from a familiar musical cue; eg guitar introduction to a familiar 'hello' song, background music played regularly at lunch time, etc.
2. Reacts spontaneously to an unfamiliar piece of music; eg rocks with innate rhythmic sense, vocalises to the sound, etc.
3. Shows spontaneous contrasting responses to different kinds of music; eg rushes round energetically to Rossini's 'William Tell Overture', sways to Rodgers and Hammerstein's 'Edelweiss'.
4. Shows controlled responses to distinct changing moods in accompanying music; eg adapts percussion playing to reflect pianist's/guitarist's sad/angry/happy playing.
5. Consciously associates a mood/emotion with a piece of music; eg gloomy: Britten's storm music from 'Sea Interludes' ('Peter Grimes'), bright: Herb Alpert's 'Spanish Flea' (Tijuana Brass), etc.
6. Recognises how playing has been adapted to convey a desired mood/emotion; eg bouncing happy music to reflect a child playing with a balloon, followed by an explosive effect and slow sad music to indicate a change in the child after the balloon burst.

Lower Key stage 1 (including nursery/reception/pupils with PMLD)

Responding to the mood of the music through an associated activity.

For example:

- Locating and tracking a sound source – to right, left, up, down, across midline to follow an intriguing sound-maker.
- Using particular pieces of music as background for regular routine activities (eg at toilet time, drinks time, lunch time, home time).
- Moving to different kinds of music, eg moving arms jerkily and smoothly to contrasting sections of a piece (aim to fade out adult support as necessary).
- Finger painting to music.
- Spontaneous dancing to music: eg class party, school disco.
- Teacher structures a basic dance: eg wheelchair dance to Gershwin's 'American in Paris' (traffic scene); pupils provide percussion accompaniment to slow-fast-slow dance.

Upper Key stage 1

Continue developing the above, in addition:

Controlled response to different kinds of music with definite contrasts.

For example:

- Playing along to musical accompaniment, adapting playing for marked loud-quiet sections.
- Contrasting two movements to match change in accompaniment: eg stamping to tambour, running to maracas.
- Sequencing two contrasting actions to illustrate dynamics through body sounds: eg slapping floor, then tapping floor with finger tips – record, listen, re-play.
- Action songs that emphasise musical elements: eg 'Dingle Dangle Scarecrow' to reinforce awareness of dynamics and silence.

Lower Key stage 2

Continue developing the above, in addition:

Structured responses to basic moods conveyed in music.

For example:

- Describing extracts of music as happy/sad/angry/scary – use smiley/sad faces etc to prompt/match as necessary.
- Using picture prompts of basic moods (happy/sad/angry/scary) to generate a mood in group playing/composing on classroom instruments.
- Using pictures of stereotyped characters – pupils to adapt playing to fit the image: eg baby, old person, athlete running, clown, soldier.
- Negative examples/inappropriate playing by teacher – pupils to correct/demonstrate suitable playing to match image as in previous example: eg teacher shouts raucously and plays loudly 'Rock-a-bye-baby'.

- Teacher structures dance involving pupils' contributions that harnesses a particular musical element, linked on a simple story idea: eg pitch: balloon inflating then bouncing along (swanee whistle – two chime bars).

Upper Key stage 2/3

Continue developing the above, in addition:

Understanding the way music is used to create a mood.

For example:

- Using an extract of music as a model for the group to create their own piece, based on a particular mood: eg Tchaikowsky's '1812 Overture' to portray explosive battle sounds.
- Participating in traditional dancing – eg samba, folk, flamenco, etc.
- Listening to a class composition (live or on tape) and adapting elements to suit an intended audience or a particular occasion: eg liven it up for a party.
- Pupils to adjust their accompaniment to extracts of music that include subtle contrasts/gradations of expression: eg 'Greensleeves' (slow/sustained), 'Kalinka' (getting faster).
- Using incidental music to convey a character through movement and/or dance: eg regal procession to Purcell's 'Trumpet Tune'.

Communicating Feelings and Ideas

Long-term aim:
To respond to and evaluate pieces of music from different cultures and traditions, using suitable forms of expression to relate to the musical elements and changing character and mood.

Short-term objectives:
1. Reacts spontaneously, demonstrating an innate positive or negative response to a distinct piece of music; eg squirms/vocalises uncomfortably at discordant playing.

2. Realises that music can be used as a channel for expression; eg identifies a class music experience captured on tape.

3. Understands that basic feelings and ideas can be encapsulated in group music-making; eg takes turn as conductor, and uses visual cues (gesture – Makaton signs or pictorial – Rebus symbols, images) to indicate how the group are to play – fast/slow, loud/quiet, happy/sad, etc.

4. Understands that ideas/feelings can be linked in a sequence to reflect a narrative or to create an effect through music; eg adapts playing to relate to images in a story board (eg three pictures in a sequence).

5. Offers an interpretation for musical ideas contained in prerecorded music/a live performance; eg invents a story-line to match a piece with contrasting sound sequences, describes the character/imagery conjured up by an evocative piece, etc.

6. Explains the intended effect conveyed in his/her own composition, with a rationale for combining sounds in a particular way; eg signs a sequence of moods to reflect a simple narrative (happy – shocked – sad, as in the balloon example above), identifies an instrument used to create a particular effect (eg cymbal as loud climax, etc).

Lower Key stage 1 (including nursery/reception/pupils with PMLD)

Reacting to a piece of music, positively and/or negatively.

For example:

- Playing music with contrasting sections in close juxtaposition (response?).
- Playing different styles of music (reactions?).
- Playing discordant/dissonant music.
- Use of familiar routine songs/music.
- Immediately re-playing pupils' sounds/music (recorded on tape).
- Use of novel sound sources: eg music technology to enhance vocalisation, through reverberation and echo.
- Playing familiar voices to pupil, pre-recorded on tape (eg teacher, mother, father, sibling, bus escort).

Upper Key stage 1

Continue developing the above, in addition:

Consciously relating to familiar sounds.

For example:

- Requesting a particular song or instrument to play.
- Recognising themselves playing instruments on tape.
- Identifying voices of class peers and familiar adults on tape.
- Using basic musical vocabulary to describe a piece of music: eg loud, quiet, fast, slow.
- Encouraging pupils to develop conscious musical taste, through presenting contrasting styles of music (on tape or in live performance) – pupils to indicate by saying/signing/gesturing yes/no which they like.

Lower Key stage 2

Continue developing the above, in addition:

Consciously relating to familiar and unfamiliar musical/sound experiences.

For example:

- Identifying more unusual/ambiguous sounds in the environment: eg helicopter whirring, whales singing, ring pulled off canned drink, etc.
- Offering ideas for musical accompaniment to part of a story: eg how to convey Jack climbing up the beanstalk, pulling out the Great Big Enormous Turnip.
- Making up a simple story with a clear beginning-middle-end, involving contrasting aspects to be conveyed on instruments: eg kitten wakes up and stretches – plays with a ball of wool – runs after a mouse.
- Listening to music with a clear structure/which conveys a story – pupils to listen for key moments: eg the cuckoo calling in the respective movement in Saint-Saëns' 'Carnival of the Animals'.

Upper Key stage 2/3

Continue developing the above, in addition:

Understanding how music can be used to express an idea or feelings.

For example:

- Painting/drawing a picture to go with a piece of music, to describe a scene – landscape, seascape, outer space, etc.
- Finding single words/short utterances to relate to a piece of music: eg 'it sounds tired', 'it's the sea', 'frightening', etc.
- Selecting an appropriate piece/extract of music to accompany a dance to convey a particular idea: eg environmental issue (river flooding).
- Considering how different composers and musicians have conveyed particular ideas and themes: eg war, the sea, the seasons, animals, space, etc.

INDIVIDUAL PROGRESS IN LISTENING TO MUSIC

Name..................

Class..................

1 → 6
begun   acquired

	Date..................
	Comments, Observations, Future Priorities
Ability to appreciate how different types of sounds are made	
Ability to appreciate how sounds are used for effect	
Ability to appreciate the cultural and historical base of pieces of music	
Ability to respond to the mood of pieces of music	
Ability to communicate feelings and ideas about pieces of music	

	Date..................
	Comments, Observations, Future Priorities
Ability to appreciate how different types of sounds are made	
Ability to appreciate how sounds are used for effect	
Ability to appreciate the cultural and historical base of pieces of music	
Ability to respond to the mood of pieces of music	
Ability to communicate feelings and ideas about pieces of music	

	Date..................
	Comments, Observations, Future Priorities

	Date..................
	Comments, Observations, Future Priorities

Resources

The list below represents a selection from the vast array of song books and resource packs to support classroom music teaching. There are many, many others which may be of interest. The following have all at certain times been useful in developing music with pupils with learning difficulties.
(*denotes cassette available **denotes video cassette accompanies text)

Baxter, K (1984) *Kit Bags* (book and instrument kits) Nottingham: NES Arnold.

Baxter, K (1993)** *Fundamental Activities* (video and book). Nottingham: Fundamental Activities.

Harrop, B (ed) and others: various song books for children, including: *Apusskidu* (1975–book of songs for piano and guitar, and classroom percussion accompaniments); *Flying a Round* (1982–rounds and partner songs); *Harlequin* (1981–songs for round the year); *Jolly Herring* (1980–folk and popular songs); *Mango Spice* (1981–Caribbean songs – reggae, calypso, ska); *Okki-Tokki-Unga* (1976–action songs for young children); *Tinder box* (1982–songs about ourselves, family and friends). All published London: A & C Black.

Harvey, E (1988)* *Jazz in the Classroom* (suggestions for developing improvised work, suitable for senior pupils with MLD). London: Boosey & Hawkes.

Hinckley, P and M (1992)* *Let's Make Music – Music for All: 1 & 2* (National Curriculum Coursework – topics for key stages 2 & 3). London: Novello & Co.

Holdstock, J and West, M (1984 – 88) *Earwiggo* (Five books produced for Yorkshire and Humberside Association for Music in Special Education): 1 *Listening Games;* 2 *Rhythm Games;* 3 *Up and Down – pitch games;* 4 *Four Chord Books;* 5 *Five Note Book* (pentatonic songs). Tadcaster: Ray Lovely Music.

Inwards, S and Paice, D (1994)* *Roundabout* (rounds to sing and ideas related to classroom topic work). Norwich: Norfolk Educational Press.

Lennard, C (1987)* *Body and Voice* (resource pack of action songs written for pupils with learning difficulties). Nottingham: LDA.

Nordoff, P (ed) (1983) *The Goldie Leigh Song Book* (music therapy songs for pupils with PMLD). London: Nordoff Robbins Music Therapy Institute.

Powell, H (1983)* *Game songs with Professor Dogg's Troupe* (interactive songs and ideas for young children). London: A & C Black.

Richards, C (1995)* *Listen to This* (suggestions for listening to music). London: Sajdix.

Thompson, D and Baxter, K (1978) *Pompaleerie Jig* (musical sound games).

Leeds: Arnold-Wheaton.

Tillman, J (1983) *Kokoleoko* (songs linked to musical elements and concepts in key stage 1). London: Macmillan.

Tillman, J (1989) *The Christmas Search* (seasonal religious and secular songs and activities). Cambridge: Cambridge Educational.

Winfield, S and Thompson, D (1991)* *Junkanoo* (easy songs from different cultures with piano and suggested percussion accompaniments). London: Universal.

Winfield, S and Thompson, D (1991)* *Whoopsey Diddley Dandy Dee* (easy songs from different cultures with piano and suggested percussion accompaniments). London: Universal.

Bibliography

(*denotes cassette tape available **denotes video accompanies text book)

Addison, R (1987) *Bright Ideas – Music*. Leamington Spa: Scholastic Publications.

Alvin, J (1965) *Music for the Handicapped Child*. London: Oxford University Press.

APMT (1988) *Music Therapy in the Education Service*. Cambridge: Association of Professional Music Therapists.

Barthorpe, T (1992) *Differentiation – Eight Ideas for the Classroom*. Scunthorpe: Desktop Publications.

Clarke, V (1991) *High, Low, Dolly Pepper*. London: A & C Black.

Davies, L (1985) *Sound Waves*. London: Bell and Hyman.

Davies, L (1993)* *Take Note!* London: BBC Educational Publishing.

Davies, L, Liebe, F and Matthews, J (1987)* *Bright Ideas – Language Resources*. Leamington Spa: Scholastic Publications.

DFE (1995) *Music in the National Curriculum*. London: HMSO.

Gilbert, J (1979) *Musical Starting Points with Young Children*. London: Ward Lock Educational.

Kempton, C 1991) *Introducing Music at Key Stage 1*. Crediton: Southgate.

Kempton, C (1992) *Developing Music at Key Stage 2*. Crediton: Southgate.

McNicholl, R (1992)** *Sound Inventions*. Oxford: Oxford University Press.

Mills, J (1991) *Music in the Primary School*. Cambridge: Cambridge University Press.

NASEN (1992) *The Music Curriculum and Special Educational Needs*. Stafford: NASEN Enterprises.

NCC (1991) *Music for ages 5-14*. York: National Curriculum Council.

NCC (1992) *Music in the National Curriculum*. York: National Curriculum Council.

NCC (1995) *The National Curriculum Orders* (draft). London: SCAA.

Nordoff, P and Robbins, C (1971) *Therapy in Music for Handicapped Children*. London: Victor Gollancz.

OFSTED (1993) *Handbook for the Inspection of Schools*. London: OFSTED.

Pelham, D and Foreman, M (1988) *Worms Wiggle*. London: Harper Collins.

Wood, M (1983) *Music for Mentally Handicapped People*. London: Souvenir Press.

York, M (1988)* *Gently into Music*. Harlow: Longman.